HANUMAN FLIES TO RAVANA'S LANKA

HANUMAN FLIES TO RAVANA'S LANKA

Lessons in Love, Humility, Devotion and Service

Kushagra Singh

Vitasta

Published by
Renu Kaul Verma
Vitasta Publishing Pvt Ltd
4348/4C, Ansari Road, Daryaganj
New Delhi - 110 002
info@vitastapublishing.com

ISBN: 978-81-19670-88-8
©Kushagra Singh
First Edition 2025
MRP ₹399

All Rights Reserved.

No part of this publication may be reproduced, stored in a retrieval system, or transmitted in any form, or by any means–electronic, mechanical, photocopying, recording or otherwise–without the prior permission of the publisher. Opinions expressed in this book are the author's own. The publisher is in no way responsible for these.

Editor: Oswald Pereira
Layout & Cover Design by Rohit Gautam
Printed by Vikas Computer and Printers, New Delhi

Contents

Introduction   vii
Acknowledgments   xiii

Embrace Your Light, Remember Your Strength   xvi-31
Nowhere to Go   1
Someone's Misery, Another's Delight   6
An Unlikely Informant   12
Mission Impossible   18
Hanu-man begins   23

Overcome Obstacles, Keep Moving Forward   32-53
Arise O Hero, Arise   33
Overcoming Distractions   38
A Test of Merit and Intelligence   43
Dealing with Negativity   48

Do Not Lose Hope   54-80
Power of Association   55
Hanuman: The Saviour of Gods   62
Stealth Mode Activated   66
Give Up, Giving   74

Proceed with Sensitivity   **82-141**
Inscrutable Destiny   83
Resilience of the Warrior Princess   89
Rama *Katha*—Antidote to Pain   101
The Most Blissful Test   109
The Game of Life   115
I Can Take You to Rama   121
Remind Rama of the Crow   128
May You Always Be Dear to Rama   134

Might of Shri Ramadoot   **142-184**
Monkeying Around   143
This Cannot be a Vanara's Work   150
Restrain Him By Any Means Possible   158
I'm an Ordinary Vanara   163
Don't Shoot the Messenger   170
Everything Burns   174
See You Soon, Ma   180

The Messenger Gets Promoted   **185-207**
Party Mode On   187
Life Saviour Hanuman   191
Ramadoot Becomes Rama Das   199
No Reason to Delay   204

Concluding Words   *209*
Suggested Reading   *215*

Introduction

In 2017, I embarked on a memorable journey from Varanasi in Uttar Pradesh to Gaya in Bihar, sharing a bus with a group of predominantly South Indian devotees and meditators. The long road between these cities was bridged not just by our travel, but also by the waves of devotion that swept through the bus. Among the various mantras and hymns that filled the air, one particular hymn struck me profoundly.

An elderly and incredibly gracious South Indian Tamilian lady began to sing the *Hanuman Chalisa*—a forty-verse hymn composed in the North Indian Awadhi dialect. Her rendition was so filled with devotion and articulated with such clear diction that everyone listened with rapt attention, including the foreigners, unfamiliar with the language, who were mesmerised by the devotion in her voice.

You might wonder what was so captivating about the lady singing the *Hanuman Chalisa*. After all, isn't this one of the first prayers that most Hindus learn as children or teenagers?

However, what left everyone spellbound was not just the hymn itself, but the inherent unity it reflected—transcending language barriers, regional differences, and, most importantly, the divisive seeds sown by history and politics. Here was a South Indian, from a region with a proud linguistic heritage, embracing a hymn in an altogether different dialect with such purity of heart that it underscored a profound truth: what binds the land of Bharat from north to south, east to west, is our universal love, devotion for our deities, and their stories, all glued together by our collective culture.

A South Indian lady blessed with a rich Tamil literary heritage of *Kambha Ramayana* and *Ramavataram* written in Tamil by a poet, Kambhar, in the 12th century on Shri Rama and Shri Hanuman, chose a devotional hymn composed in Awadhi by Tulsidas. This beautifully illustrates the transcendental nature of spiritual expression in Bharat. It is also a living testament to the universal appeal and enduring charm of Shri Tulsidas's composition and to the universal reverence held for Shri Hanuman, whose glory often seems to eclipse even that of his Lord, Shri Rama.

Reflecting on Hanuman's character, it is pertinent to recall Shri Rama's observations when he met Hanuman for the first time, as recorded in the *Kishkindhā Kānda*:

'No one who is not learned in Rigveda, Yajurveda, and Samaveda can speak like how Hanuman has spoken. His speech was concise, clear, without delay, without tremor and was spoken in medium tone. He spoke so much, but not one word was amiss. He sounded like one who is well-learned in *vyakarana* (grammar). His speech was refined and coherent. He spoke words that were auspicious and pleasing to the heart. There was no flaw noticeable on his face or eyes or his forehead or anywhere else. He is so well-spoken that his words will enchant even an enemy who is ready to attack him with his sword raised.' (*Kishkindhā Kānda* 4.3.28–4.3.34.)

While the entire Ramayana narration is divine and glorious, the fifth part, known as *Sundara Kanda* is exceptional. Well, it is actually the fifth part that is sung and recited most often in gatherings of devotees or meditated on by *bhakti* yogis. Sundara Kanda is the part of Ramayana where the great Valmiki introduces the reader to Hanuman's glories and greatness.

The *Sundara Kanda* is cherished across spiritual traditions for profound reasons:

Devotees facing adverse planetary influences like those from Saturn and Mars often seek refuge in Sundara Kanda; Shri Ramadoot's blessings is believed to shield against the malefic effects of any planet, providing divine protection to those in distress.

Bhakti Yogis celebrate the Sundara Kanda for showcasing Shri Hanuman's exemplary devotion to Lord Rama. It reinforces the belief that with deep faith, no challenge is too great, echoing Tulsidas's words, '*More man as prabhu biswasa, Ram tay adhik Ram kar dasa*—Greater than Rama is Rama's servant.'

For *Advait Vedantins*, Hanuman's journey symbolises the union of the individual soul (Sita) with the supreme soul (Shri Rama), overcoming the ego (Ravana). This is a powerful allegory for spiritual enlightenment through unwavering devotion.

Drawing from the profound legacy of the Ramayana and my veneration for Shri Ramadoot Hanuman, I was inspired to pen this book. I thus hope to make a modest contribution to Shri Rama's boundless glory and the the Lord's majestic messenger. I have endeavoured to remain true to Maharishi Valmiki's original masterpiece, while adding some enriching details from Tulsi Ramayan and folklores.

My approach steers clear of the contemporary trend of adapting sacred scriptures for mere entertainment, which often risks diminishing their spiritual essence. Instead, I aim to present the authentic epic in accessible language, interspersed with personal reflections and the insights bestowed upon me by my gurus and devout devotees of Bhagavan Shri Rama.

This book is not just a passage through an ancient story but a journey of personal growth and spiritual enrichment. As you delve deeper into the book, you will find that it intricately weaves stories within stories, each designed to captivate your mind and expand your understanding of life's deeper truths. Our rich Indian heritage, as encapsulated in texts like the Ramayana and the Mahabharata, offers endless wisdom, presenting new lessons with each reading.

Each chapter is crafted to follow a consistent structure: an engaging narrative followed by a section titled 'Key Takeaway' where I share the lessons drawn from the tale. This is complemented by 'Your Reflections,' a segment designed to prompt introspection and personal growth, echoing the venerable practice of श्रवण और मनन—listening/reading and reflecting.

I would also recommend that you set an intention before you read this book. It is my sincere belief that anyone who reads the epic tale of Shri Rama and his messenger and meditates on the learnings will be bestowed with spiritual power, strength, glory, prosperity, and success in life.

This book is a tribute to that enthusiastic child within me, fulfilling a dream to celebrate and share the glory of Ramayana that I cherished since my earliest days. My sincere prayer and wish is that my reflections on this epic inspire you to overcome your fears and doubts, and through the blessings of Shri Rama, may you be filled with hope, positivity, and joy.

बुद्धिहीन तनु जानिके सुमिरौं पवन कुमार
बल बुद्धि बिद्या देहु मोहिं हरहु कलेस बिकार

Fully aware of the deficiency of my intelligence, I concentrate my attention on Pavan Kumar and humbly ask for strength, intelligence and true knowledge to relieve me of all blemishes, causing pain.

Kushagra Singh

Acknowledgments

I cannot proceed without expressing my gratitude to the people who have inspired, helped, supported, and guided me in my writing journey.

First of all, this book is the direct result of Bhagavan Shri Krishna's grace. Without his blessings, support, inspiration, and nudge, I cannot achieve anything remotely of significance, let alone this book. Anything good that you find within the pages of this book is the manifestation of the grace of my sweet master, lord, and guide, Parameshwar Shri Krishna.

Some say that Shri Krishna was the first personality who in one way, initiated someone into worship of Hanuman. The ever-smiling Lord had asked his friend and disciple to seek blessings from Hanuman before the great war of Kurukshetra.

Legend also says that during the end of the war, Krishna explains to Arjuna that the reason his chariot didn't crumble against the relentless attack by the Kaurava army was because Hanuman's image was imprinted on the flag atop the chariot.

I thank Shri Maha Ganapati, son of the great Bhagavan Shiva

and Ma Parvati, who is the bestower of refined intelligence and wisdom needed to churn out this book.

I thank the Devi of learning and education, Ma Saraswati, for inspiring words to flow to form a book.

I thank my father, Shri Anil Kumar Singh, for his continued blessings, support and nudge to keep up my writing journey and not worry about the results.

I thank Sheetal and Saurin for their immense support, encouragement, and feedback to help me gain the confidence to write more.

I thank Mukund Hari Prabhu and Mansi Mataji for their prayers, support and blessings.

I thank my dear friends, Rohit Gautam, Rizwan (and Mrs Rizwan) and Abhijeet for their continued support in my writing journey.

Archana Kumar is another friend who has always been a tremendous force of support. Roma Lakhani is always a wise friend to seek ideas and opinions.

I thank my brother, Abhinav Singh, for reading and promoting my work. Thank you to the very inspiring Sandhya Gola for her support.

Shreya (the gimli) has been incredibly kind in her words and encouragement.

Poorak Varma, Vidhi Bhabhi, Sudhanshu Sethi have all been friends who live far away but are close to the heart and keep encouraging and supporting.

Thank you to Priti for the first-ever review of my first book.

Special thanks to Miss Anulata Raj Nair, the first person to write me a 'fan mail' after my first book. Those words of appreciation from a (relative) stranger meant the world.

Thank you to Aparna Sahai, and Prabhav for their love and kindness.

Thank you to Praveen, Divyakshi, and Tanishka for turning up at my first-ever book launch and your kind love.

Thank you to Mehak Dua, Aditi and Sravan, Nandini, Megha, Prateek, Anupriya for their support. Thank you to Vipul Kalra, Gautami, Ekta for engaging with my work. Thanks as well to Prachi and Richa.

Thank you to Gaurangi Mangal and Bhakti Bhosale for their love and support.

Thank you to Madhu Madhav Prabhu for placing my first book at the lotus feet of my venerable Vrindavan Behari Jee. Thank you to Abhay Gauranga Prabhu for your prayers and love.

Thank you to Abhishek Joshi sir and Priyanka ma'am for helping me grow as a person.

Thank you to Gaurav Sharma, Siddharth Gupta, Namrata, Sukriti, Priyanka, Aniruddh, Nidhi and Manash, Raghav Suri, Dr Pooja, Devanshi, Deepak Yadav, Pratibha, Adeeba, Anjali Pandey, Akshat, Pragati, Ishita, Harshita, Ish Gupta Prabhu, Nishant, Krittika Shukla, Veenakshi, Pragya, Roma Singh, Aryan for their encouragement.

Surabhi Sankhe's mesmerising sketches help the readers visualise events from the tale. I thank her for her brilliant creative work.

Thanks to Padhega India for promoting my first book and for distributing it as well.

The book could find a home in Vitasta, thanks to the efforts and guidance of Lipika Bhushan. Your feedback, suggestions and kindness has been of tremendous help.

Thank you to Renu Kaul Verma, Managing Director of Vitasta Publishing, for giving a newbie author like me a platform to share his work. Special thanks to Oswald for his editorial suggestions.

Lastly, thank you to all the kind souls who read and reviewed my first book.

Section 1

Embrace Your Light, Remember Your Strength

Chapter 1

Nowhere to Go

The word *Va-nara*, as mentioned by sage Valmiki in the Ramayana, literally can be defined as, *'Are you human?'*

Vanaras were a special race of people, who, despite their simian-like appearance, possessed wondrous strength and capabilities. They were not monkeys in the literal sense, as is often misunderstood. The Vanaras had their own kingdom at Kishkindha and many illustrious souls were part of their clan. The scriptures also reveal that many gods had taken the form of Vanaras to assist Bhagavan Shri Vishnu in his human pastime as Shri Rama, in his mission to annihilate the demoniac Ravana.

Sugreeva, the king of the Vanara army, had sent different units of his army in all directions to help Shri Rama locate his wife, Devi Sita. In his past, he had been forced to flee from his estranged brother Vali, who was vengeful and sought his life. Sugreeva's extensive knowledge of the world allowed him to provide detailed coordinates and route guidance for each direction to his army.

He entrusted his most trusted and capable generals to go in the southern direction. This was so because it was suspected that the demoniac Ravana had abducted Sita and taken her somewhere down south. And hence, *warriors like Angad, wise old bear king Jambavan, Nala, Nila, and, of course, our very own Hanuman were part of the unit that went southwards.*

With a sense of urgency, each retinue of the army was given a month to return with concrete information on Sita's whereabouts. The consequences of failure were dire, as they would face the wrath of Sugreeva. As the deadline neared, the retinue was nowhere close to finding any clue about Devi Sita's whereabouts, heightening the tension and anticipation.

As luck would have it, one day on their journey, they spotted an entrance to a vast cave. The Vanaras, weary from their search and hopeful for a respite, noticed birds flying out of the cave, their wings wet as if they'd been dipped in water. With a glimmer of hope in their hearts, they formed a chain and decided to enter the cave, anticipating a much-needed food and water break.

The cave seemed to transport them to another world. The cave sparkled with gems, couches, and giant trees surrounded by ponds filled with clear water.

The magical cave provided the weary army with fruits and beverages to rejuvenate them. The long and arduous search had been both physically and mentally taxing.

The cave's guardian, a mystical yogini named Swayamprabha, had arranged food when she learnt about their sacred mission of assisting Lord Rama. Her presence brought a sense of calm and reassurance to the Vanaras, who were grateful for her aid. While Swayamprabha did provide food and drinks and aided in their safe exit from the cave, it did little to alleviate their anxiety about finding Devi Sita. In fact, as they were transported out of the cave to the beautiful vista of the southern ocean, their anxiety soared. The vastness of the ocean and the uncertainty of their mission weighed heavily on their hearts.

More than a month's time had already passed since the party had begun the mission. It now appeared they had reached a definite dead end. Completely out of their wits, seeds of dissension started brewing within the army.

Key Takeaway
Learning from the Past

We never know when something that happened to us in the past may turn into a blessing. Rather, we can utilise each situation and occurrence in life consciously—if not for our own good, perhaps for someone else, as it happens in the case of Sugreeva.

Sugreeva had to run for his dear life when his brother, Vali, assumed to be dead, returned out of the blue and suspected Sugreeva of conspiring against him. Scared for his life, Sugreeva had to desperately search for a safe hiding place. At long last, he found a safe location at *Rishyamukha* mountain, which was out of bounds for Vali due to an earlier curse upon him.

When Sugreeva started sending his army in all four directions, his elaborate explanation of topography and geography stunned Shri Rama. When Lord Rama queried Sugreeva about this, he revealed the reason for his profound knowledge—it was out of necessity rather than interest!

Using Sugreeva's example, all of us can also choose to frame a past experience, even if bitter, as something that may turn out to be useful. If not immediately, then later; if not for us, maybe for someone else.

After all, is there a more remarkable teacher than experience?

As the popular Hindi proverb goes:

'अकल बादाम खाने से नहीं आती, तजुर्बे से आती है'

Your Reflection

What is that one experience in your life, though bitter, felt like a blessing later on?

Chapter 2

Someone's Misery, Another's Delight

The situation was dire.

Angad, the prince of Kishkindha and the appointed leader of the southern retinue of Kishkindha's army that had left in search of Devi Sita, was now losing hope. As often happens with so many of us, in testing times, our spirit starts to wither away. And as hope and spirit wane, it is replaced by negative and toxic thoughts. Angad was no exception.

The beautiful vista of the endless shores of the ocean and the clear blue skies above, which ordinarily bring peace and tranquillity, was inducing a sense of unease and anxiety among the Vanara army.

Angad started lamenting about their failure to find Devi Sita. Recalling Sugreeva's deadline, he feared that their failure would surely result in their execution by the king when they returned to their homeland. Rather than dying a shameful death in front of their family, Angad said, 'I'd prefer to sit here and fast unto death, than go back and be executed.'

The prince's idea to rather die here than return with unpleasant news of their failure was met with approval by some within the army. Some suggested a return to the magical cave and to relish the pleasures there until the end of their time.

Shri Hanuman stepped in to remind Angad that he will always be treated with kindness and respect by his uncle. He spoke about Sugreeva's even-mindedness to Angad and his mother, Tara. He also sternly reminded the Vanaras of the absolutely destructive power and prowess of Rama and Lakshmana's arrows. Vayuputra Hanuman suggested they all return to the kingdom, share an honest report of their expedition, and wait for further instructions.

Angad's current negative state of mind was inflamed by hearing Hanuman's words of wisdom. The feelings of anger and hate that had seeped into him when his father had died re-emerged.

Angad felt Sugreeva was an ungrateful person who had usurped his father's kingdom, got his father killed, and even forgotten the favours of Lord Rama after becoming the king. It was only Lakshmana's stern reminder that spurred Sugreeva to begin the search for Devi Sita's location.

To briefly give a little context to Angad's rant, Vali, Angad's father, and Sugreeva were brothers. During a battle away from the kingdom, misjudging that Vali had died battling a demon, Sugreeva locked Vali up in a cave. Sugreeva was made the king in his elder brother's absence, but Vali returned one day, bashed and shamed Sugreeva, and even took away his wife. Vali did not even allow Sugreeva to explain his actions but cemented enmity between them.

Later, when Lord Rama killed Vali, Angad's mentorship was handed over to Rama by his dying father. In his last moments, Vali realised his follies and sought forgiveness for his mistakes. Lord Rama got Angad installed as the prince regent of Kishkindha.

Angad's condition is a classic case of unhealed emotions surfacing when we are confronted with intense challenges. Angad trusted the wisdom of his dying father to surrender himself under the guidance and protection of Bhagavan Rama. While Angad understood why his father had to be killed and did not harbour any negativity against Shri Rama, his attitude towards Sugreeva was different.

The entire situation of his uncle returning as the king, seeing him in place of his father on the throne, as well as the idea that had already been entrenched in his mind that his uncle had tricked his father for the throne induced a lot of angst in Angad's heart.

I am sure you also must have observed that often negative thoughts spiral when our external situations get challenging. In such times, I pray we have the sage company of someone like our hero, Shri Hanuman, who can speak words of wisdom rather than adding fuel to the burning fire of negativity.

On expressing his feelings, Angad broke down and declared he would fast unto death rather than return back to his kingdom. Angad's heart was in a state of deep anguish, for the young and spirited warrior felt shattered at what seemed like a failed mission.

Along with Angad, most of the other members of the Vanara army sat down to wait for inevitable death to consume them. They too, feared returning back empty-handed.

While the Vanaras sat down, an aged and gigantic vulture observing this scene from a nearby cave chuckled at how Providence was preparing a feast for him!

As it is said, *one's misery can often mean another's delight.*

Noticing the vulture express delight at their misery, Angad said that the vulture must be a representative of Yamaraj; Yama, the god of death must have come to end their lives, for they failed in their mission to serve Lord Rama. Angad reflected that the bird reminded him of the pious and brave Jatayu, who had died trying to protect Devi Sita from the demoniac and cowardly Ravana.

The mention of Jatayu's bravery and sacrifice stirred a profound change in the vulture's demeanour. From a predator eagerly awaiting a feast, it transformed into a sorrowful creature, shedding tears and urging the Vanaras to share more about Jatayu.

What was the connection between Jatayu and this gigantic bird, and how did the predator turn into an informer and guide?

Key Takeaway
Find Your Inner Peace

While our surroundings definitely do play a significant role in shaping our frame of mind, they are not always the ultimate factor in determining it. More often than not, how one feels internally can overcome the power of external influences.

Even the most mundane places can be a memorable experience to visit when we are happy and in good company; even the most picturesque locations can do little to enhance our mood if there are more pressing concerns on our minds.

In other words, as we see here, the beautiful surroundings in which the Vanara army found themselves did little to ease their anxiety—rather, it accentuated it.

This in itself serves as a powerful lesson for us—our surroundings and external situations cannot bring peace to us unless there is peace and contentment within the mind and the heart space.

Our modern lifestyle, science, and applied sciences stress extensively on creating a comfortable outer environment and precious little on enhancing the inner space. While appreciating and benefiting from the achievements of science and technology, there is an immense need to address how we can keep our inner world pleasant.

Your Reflection
Just like Angad, is there something you need to address and heal from your past?

Is there someone we need to forgive and release the load from our heart and mind?

Chapter 3

An Unlikely Informant

Jatayu and Sampati were powerful vulture birds. The siblings were offsprings of Aruna, the charioteer of the Sun deity. The might, strength, valour, and confidence of the two mystical birds knew no bounds.

In Vedic scriptures, all the planets, along with the sun and moon are personified and understood to be presided over by a deity. For instance, Shri Krishna mentions the name Vivasvan in the fourth chapter of the Bhagavad Gita to be the presiding deity of the sun.

It is also mentioned in various Vedic literature texts that the offspring of the gods are not always human-like, but also end up taking the form of various animal forms. While the offsprings of the gods may resemble earthly creatures (humans included), their strength and power far exceeds that of earthly mortals.

Emboldened by their strength and driven by the recklessness of youth, one day eons ago, both the brothers decided to soar towards the sun. The planned adventure turned into a tragedy as the birds couldn't handle the intense sun rays. While falling down, Sampati nestled his brother Jatayu in his wings so he was protected. However, Sampati's wings got burned, and he was crippled for life. More than the physical pain, the anguish of being separated from his brother ailed Sampati. He continued to live by the grace and kindness of a sage named Nishakara.

The sage's aura was such that all animals, even the most violent ones, became peaceful in his presence. He was kind and loving to all creatures, and all animals near the vicinity considered him to be like a father figure. Sampati was fortunate he had fallen near the sage's ashram, who then nursed him back to health.

Hearing the mention of his dear brother Jatayu after such a long time brought tears to the eyes of the gigantic but crippled vulture Sampati—the one who had been observing the monkeys sitting in a cave. He implored Angad and the other Vanaras to speak more about his brother.

Did he hear them correctly…had his dearest brother really perished?

Angad shared the story about the glorious death of Jatayu, who fought the cowardly Ravana to prevent him from kidnapping Devi Sita. Angad revealed the reason why the Vanaras had come to the southern shores. He requested Sampati to aid and assist in any clue or help in locating Ravana's abode and Devi Sita's whereabouts.

Sampati revealed that the sage who had nursed him back to health had made a prophecy that one day an army of Vanaras would come looking for Sita. If Sampati helped them out, he would completely heal and be free from suffering.

Sampati shared an incident that had happened years ago. He said one day, he had heard the loud wails of a Yaksha woman (Yakshas are celestial beings being presided over by Kubera, the god of wealth). The woman was being carried off by a demon in a plane. Sampati had obstructed the flight and had a minor duel with the demon. In spite of his crippled condition, Sampati did cause a dent to the demon's body and ego. The demon revealed himself to be the king of demons, Ravana. He let the woman go but struck a pact with the gigantic bird that from now on, the bird will never obstruct his path, and in turn the demons would never trouble the bird.

The incident happened years ago when Sampati was younger. Now, he was weaker and utterly dependent upon his son Suparshava's services for survival. And Suparshava too, a few months ago, had an encounter with the demon king.

Sampati revealed that Suparshava had seen the demon king flying down south with a lady who constantly cried out for help and was taking the name of Rama and Lakshmana. Suparshava flew over to the plane, but the cowardly Ravana begged him to let him go. Sampati reckoned that owing to his previous encounters with the gigantic vultures, Ravana did not want to duel with a younger bird again. Sampati rued his son's misplaced compassion but promised to aid the Vanaras in locating Devi Sita.

As soon as Sampati uttered his intention of helping out the Vanaras, his injured and incapacitated limbs started healing, and new wings sprouted out, replacing his useless ones. The Vanaras were wonderstruck with such a miracle unfolding in front of their eyes. With renewed vitality of body and mind, the gigantic vulture Sampati, who had the unique ability to view objects hundreds of kilometres away, scanned the southern shores attentively and revealed:

'About 100 *yojanas* (1 *yojana* is approximately 12 kilometres) from here, Sita is held captive on the island of Lanka. She is fiercely guarded by *rakshashis* (demonesses). One of you should go to the place and ascertain the exact location and take the information back to Shri Rama.'

Fulfilling his destiny and role in the play of life and bidding adieu and luck to the Vanara army, the gigantic bird flew away.

The Vanaras felt like they were given a reprieve of life by the divine! It was like a rebirth amidst the fog of uncertainty clouding their minds, hearts and most importantly, spirit.

To find and establish the concrete location of Devi Sita, all the Vanaras had to do was cross the 100 *yojanas* long ocean and voila!

Oh wait…what did Sampati say, cross the 100-*yojana* long ocean!

Can anyone dare to take upon this seemingly impossible mission? Was there anyone amidst the Vanaras who was capable of not just crossing the great ocean but also finding a way to enter the heavily protected island, and kingdom of the demons?

Key Takeaway
Have Faith in the Divine
The readers of Harry Potter must be familiar with the famous words of Dumbledore, 'You will find that help will always be given at Hogwarts to those who ask for it.'

Along similar lines, help will always be provided to us by the divine in the most unlikeliest of ways, if we are focused on a positive goal and mission in life. Perhaps our goal and mission may not be as big as the one concerning the selfless Vanaras who were serving Shri Rama, but on the cosmic scale, nothing is big or small. We need to cultivate faith and belief that no matter what, help will always come, and we should not lose hope in the face of challenges and adversity.

You might say all this is easier said than done. But that is why we have stories; we have *itihaas* or history, as the tale of Ramayan is called in Vedic parlance.

Unlike modern day history, *itihaas* simply does not recount the chronological events and dates of the past, but rather it is a living tale that uses historical accounts to deliver timeless lessons. Such tales uplift our dwindling spirits and ensure we remain motivated.

As we move along the story, you will find incredible lessons and tips to overcome adversity, gain strength and a resolute purpose to grow in life.

Your Reflection
Journal about a time when you received help from the most unlikeliest of sources, and in the most unexpected manner.

Chapter 4

Mission Impossible

The Vanara army, their emotions oscillating like a sine wave, was on the verge of a crucial discovery.

Divine (and gigantic bird Sampati's vision) intervention had helped them establish a clue about Devi Sita's location. But now the question was about scaling that distance.

And it wasn't just any ordinary location. One doesn't have to just deal with pangs of hunger, navigate an arduous terrain, and so on. Now, someone needs to jump or fly across the vast expanse of the southern ocean—a distance of around 1,200 kilometres—enter the extensively guarded abode of the extremely powerful *rakshasas* or demons, and establish conclusive evidence of Sita's presence.

And nope, no ferries or chartered flights available either. Even Ethan Hunt (Tom Cruise) may have had to hold his hands up and say, this one is truly mission impossible!

Prince Angad, undeterred by the seemingly insurmountable task, rallied the Vanara army. 'We have a lead,' he declared, 'and it's time to see who among us can bridge the distance to the island of Lanka.'

Sheepishly, some Vanaras began speaking of their estimation

of how far they could leap. None had either the capability or confidence to leap the distance to Lanka. As a responsible leader, Angad spoke up and revealed he could leap the hundred *yojana* distance, but, he had doubts about being able to return. Angad's proclamation was met with cheers by the Vanara army. But his admission of having doubts about returning cast a shadow of uncertainty over their hearts.

Scholars of the Ramayana point out here that Angad's admission of having doubts about returning was less about his physical ability and more about the mind. Lanka was known to be a place where materialism was at its peak. Angad was well aware that without the guiding light of mentors such as Jambavan around him, he may find himself lost in the sparkle of materialism and forget his mission altogether.

Jambavan, a sagely and powerful chief of the bear army, spoke up. He was of the opinion that regardless of capability, Angad, being the prince regent and the leader should not be the one to undertake the mission. He reckoned someone else in the Vanara army had to fulfil this mission.

Jambavan became nostalgic about his personal capabilities. He recounted with pride how in his youth, he had circled the globe twenty-one times, announcing to one and all the news of Sri Vamana Bhagavan's (an incarnation of Shri Vishnu Bhagavan) victory over the great King Bali. His past achievements were a testament to his wisdom and experience. Jambavan had been alive since eons and had seen different ages, as per Vedic calculations. In his current state and age it was not possible for him to scale and leap the 100 yojana distance.

While all others were engaged in discussion about their capabilities and who could complete the mission, *one person* sat away as if in a trance.

Jambavan asked Hanuman, 'Why are you silent, O mighty son of Vayu (wind god)? I know you possess tremendous strength and ability.'

Hanuman had not revealed his prowess or how far he could leap. But Jambavan knew more about Hanuman's capabilities better than anyone else present there—even more than Hanuman himself!

The Vanara army was now all ears, their curiosity piqued by the wise old bear's words. What was the secret about Shri Hanuman that none of them knew? The air was thick with anticipation. Thus, Jambavan began narrating the history and making of one of the most cherished, iconic, and venerable figures in Sanatana Dharma.

Key Takeaway
Recognise Another's Potential

In a group, the person who speaks the most is assumed to be a leader and often takes up leadership roles. Often, the voice, abilities, and talent of introverts and those who speak less go unnoticed. A good leader should be the one who can extract the best ideas, identify potential, and put the larger interest above his personal ego.

Here, Sri Jambavan is a textbook example of an amazing leader. He identifies Hanuman's potential, amidst many other soldiers. Despite Hanuman's silence, Jambavan ensures that his abilities are brought to the fore.

Also, a word of appreciation for Angad. The spirited young prince was so self-aware and humble that he could admit his doubts about returning from Lanka. Angad had been appointed the leader of the group, and for a leader to lead with honesty, exemplifying self-awareness will always extract the best from the group.

Your Reflection

Have you come across any shy, or reticent person around you, who later turned out to be a person blessed with immense talent? Is there any ability or talent that you possess, but are too shy to share with others?

Chapter 5

Hanu-man begins

There are many versions and stories about the appearance of our hero, Shri Hanuman.

In the Valmiki Ramayana, there's a brief yet profound description of Hanuman's birth. Jambavan recounts how Vayu—the wind god, was captivated by a celestial damsel known as Punjikasthala. Their union was blessed with the prophecy that she would one day give birth to an illustrious and glorious son, a being of unparalleled strength, equal to the wind god himself.

However, in various other scriptures and resources, we encounter diverse versions of Hanuman's divine appearance. In this chapter, I will delve into these unique and different narratives, highlighting that the birth of our hero was divinely ordained.

Anand Ramayana Version

In the Anand Ramayana, Hanuman was believed to be born from the blessing of the divine Yajna or the fire ceremony that was conducted by King Dasrath in Ayodhya. Dasrath Maharaj conducted a Vedic fire ceremony under the guidance of the great Sage Shringa to attain the blessing of an offspring. On completion of the ritual, a celestial being appeared with a pot of *kheer* (a sweet pudding). Dasrath Maharaj had fed that divine food to his chief queens, and thus, they were blessed with four great sons—Shri Rama, Bharat, Lakshmana, and Shatrughna. It is described how a bird (actually the wind god in the form of a bird) grabbed a portion of that *kheer* and dropped it in the palms of a meditating female Vanara Anjana's lap— who upon consuming it, gave birth to Hanuman.

The blessings and grace of Bhagavan Shiva arranged for this serendipity as Anjana had been worshipping Him with the desire to be blessed with a son for a long time. Pleased by her devotion, the great Bholenath had blessed her that the eleventh *Rudra* would be born to her.

Shiva Purana Version
Once, Ma Parvati asked Bhagavan Shiva why did he keep repeating the name 'Rama.' Bhagavan Shiva replied that the name of Rama was a potent mantra, and it had manifested itself in the form of an earthly prince and happened to be an incarnation of Bhagavan Vishnu.

The great lord of dissolution, Shiva, further said he now wanted to incarnate in the earthly realm to serve the mission of Shri Vishnu. Upon Ma Parvati's protest, Shiva said he would only send a part of his energy (अंश). Chandrashekhar Shiva decided to appear as a Vanara to lead a simple lifestyle away from societal norms to enable him to serve more. Ma Parvati, too, appeared with Shiva as Hanuman's tail. Hence Hanuman's tail was exquisitely beautiful. So, in that way, Shri Hanuman is the manifestation of both Shiva and Shakti!

Another story comes in the Shiva Purana, where Vayu helped Bhagavan Shiva in a battle against the demoniac Jalandhara.

Pleased with Vayu's help, the almighty Shiva offered him a boon, and Vayu asked him to be born as his son.

Bhagavan Vishnu had also prayed to Shiva to help him slay Ravana and offered him red lotus flowers, with a thousand petals each. Bhagavan Shiva informed Shri Vishnu that He had already so blessed Anjana that he would be born to her, and that His incarnation would undoubtedly help Shri Rama.

Mohini and Shiva

Srimad Bhagavatam mentions that Bhagavan Shiva wanted to see the feminine incarnation of Bhagavan Shri Vishnu. On his request, when the Lord of Maya, Shri Vishnu revealed His Mohini form, even the great ascetic Shiva fell for her.

Bhagavan Shiva's potent and divine seed got ejaculated as He ran after Mohini—that seed was preserved by the Saptarishis (seven great sages). Eventually this seed was slipped into a meditative Anjana's ear (and in her womb) by Vayu.

And so, Hanuman is known as an incarnation of Shiva, son of Vayu, and also Kesari Nandan (Kesari was his Vanara father), as all of these personalities had a role in the manifestation of Hanuman.

Baby Anjaneya is named Hanuman

As a baby, Anjaneya, son of Mother Anjana, had a seemingly insatiable appetite. No matter how many fruits and roots were fed to the baby, his hunger would not satiate.

One day, as Ma Anjana was busy with some chores, baby Anjaneya saw what appeared to be a nice, big *fruit* nestled amidst a tall tree. Not wanting to bother his parents, who were constantly pressured by the demands of the baby Anjaneya, he decided to be independent and leapt towards the fruit.

Aided and assisted by the adoring father Vayu, Anjaneya was

flying towards the solar deity unabated. Even Surya Dev did not allow his rays to cause harm to the baby as he was aware of his divine origins.

Coincidentally, the day Anjaneya leapt towards the sun was a day of solar eclipse. Vedic understanding of eclipse is that *Rahu, the body-less entity tries to devour Surya and Chandra* (moon god) due to an enmity* created during the great churning of the ocean.

When baby Anjaneya saw another round-shaped figure near the bigger fruit, he diverted his attention towards Rahu. Rahu got scared for his life and rushed towards Indra—the king of the heavens, and complained that some powerful creature was inhibiting Rahu from following his duty.

Indra arrived on the scene, and once again, baby Anjaneya mistook Indra's aura and radiance to be that of a fruit!

As Anjaneya leapt towards Indra, he was struck by the thunderbolt weapon or the *Vajra* of Indra. The weapon struck baby Anjaneya on his chin and rendered him unconscious. Anjaneya started free-falling from the heavens, but was saved and carried back to the earthly realm by Vayu.

Vayu was consumed by grief and anger at Indra's impunity to strike his baby boy. He withdrew the life air from all of the universe. On sensing the danger to every living creature, the creator Brahma along with other deities, appeared to meet Vayu and baby Anjaneya. Brahma did not just revive the baby back to life, but he, and all the other prominent deities, poured innumerable blessings on baby Hanuman.

Indra put a garland of lotus flowers around Anjaneya's neck and named him Hanuman (one with a disfigured chin on being hit by the Vajra). He also made Anjaneya invulnerable to his weapon henceforth.

Surya—bestowed a part of his radiance on the baby. He also promised to be Hanuman's teacher when his time for education arrived. He blessed Hanuman that none will be superior to him in the knowledge of the scriptures and Vedas.

Varuna—the god of water blessed Hanuman that he would never have any fear of water.

Agni—the fire god, blessed Hanuman to be invulnerable to fire.

Yama—the god of death blessed that baby Hanuman would be immune to diseases and could choose the time of his death.

Kubera—blessed Hanuman to remain forever energised during a battle.

Bhagavan Shiva—blessed His avatar to be a Chiranjeevi or an immortal.

Vishwakarma—the divine architect gave him immunity against all kinds of weapons.

Lord Brahma—blessed that Hanuman would be immune to the destructive power of the *Brahmastra*. Lord Brahma further said that Hanuman would be invincible in battle. He would terrorise his evil foes and free people from fear. Hanuman was also blessed to be able to change his form at will and go wherever he pleased at the speed of his choice. Brahma blessed Hanuman with a victory boon that ensured that all of Hanuman's activities will turn out to be glorious.

Bhagavan Vishnu—blessed Hanuman to be a great devotee. He mentioned how Hanuman would be like a brother to him in his Rama avatar.

All gods pronounced that there would be none in heaven or earth, equal in strength and speed to Hanuman.

Brahma concluded the gathering by further blessing him to be greater in strength and speed even to Vayu and Garuda (the carrier of Lord Vishnu).

Ecstatic at the extraordinary blessings received by his son,

Vayu revived all living beings, and carried Anjaneya back to his earthly parents—Anjana and Kesari. Vayu Dev then narrated the episode to Shri Hanuman's parents and informed them of all the blessings received by their dear child.

Mischievous Child is Cursed (Blessed)

Armed with innumerable divine blessings and spurred on by the naughty proclivity of childhood, Hanuman started playing pranks on people in his vicinity. Even as a child, Anjaneya loved the company of saints, sages and yogis. He would not only seek to be around them, soaking their peaceful, and loving aura, but also loved to make them a target of his mischief!

Pulling their beards, soiling their clothes, breaking their sacrificial ladles and vessels were some of the ways in which he would bother the saints.

Despite repeated checks by his parents, Hanuman did not abate his mischief. Finally, wanting to rein in the mischief and keeping in mind Hanuman's divine purpose of appearance, one advanced yogi put a curse on Hanuman—this child will forget all his divine powers. They will only return to him when they are most needed, and when reminded of them.

Uncle Ben, in the origin story of the iconic comic book character Spiderman, utters a legendary line: 'With great power comes great responsibility.'

There cannot be a better context for Hanuman forgetting his powers as a child. Great power, if left unchecked and used unconsciously, can lead to havoc. Great power must always be married to a divine purpose of creating greater good for society.

As Jambavan concluded his narration of Hanuman's past, the time for Hanuman to embrace his divinity in toto had arrived. The wise bear king Jambavan's words lifted the restriction on Vayuputra's powers. The meditative and silent Hanuman suddenly started expanding in size.

कवन सो काज कठिन जग माहीं । जो नहिं होइ तात तुम्ह पाहीं । ।
राम काज लगि तव अवतारा । सुनतहिं भयउ पर्बताकारा । ।
(*Ramacharitmanas* by Goswami Tulsidas)

'There is no task that you cannot accomplish, O Son. You have appeared to fulfil Shri Rama's mission— as soon as Hanuman heard this, He expanded his body to mountainous proportions.'

---

*When nectar appeared during the churning of the cosmic ocean, Shri Vishnu appeared as Mohini and tricked the demons and fed the *amrita* or nectar of immortality to the gods. Rahu somehow managed to conceal himself and get a portion of the nectar before getting his head chopped off by Lord Vishnu's Sudarshan Chakra. Because Rahu had tasted the nectar, he retained his consciousness and lives on as a celestial being, while only retaining his head. Rahu is considered as an important planet in Vedic astrology.

Key Takeaway
We all Need a Jambavan

In my last book, *Wisdom From The Smiling Panda*, I wrote a chapter, 'We all need a Jambavan,' glorifying Sri Jambavan. In a way, it is Jambavan who turns out to be the *MVP* (most valued person) in the war against Ravana. He was the one who inspired Hanuman to leap across the vast ocean, reach Lanka, and ascertain Devi Sita's whereabouts.

As one of my spiritual teachers, Vraj Bihari Das, says, 'We have so many temples dedicated to Shri Hanuman, but how many temples are dedicated to Jambavan?'

The most significant lesson I want to draw your attention to, dear reader, is the importance of wise mentors and good company in our life journey.

Jambavan signifies that wise mentor who helps us realise our untapped, hidden potential. He sees our ability and helps us believe in it even when we do not. He also advises us about the value of having wise people in our lives, who offer sage counsel and never let us lose hope.

Your Reflection

First, do you have a Jambavan-like mentor in your life? If yes, have you acknowledged his or her contribution to your life? If not, please do so.

Second, how can you be a Jambavan for someone else?

Far too often we are looking for someone like Jambavan and seeking to be glorious like Hanuman. What is needed more is that we become like Jambavan and help uplift others.

Section 2

Overcome Obstacles, Keep Moving Forward

Chapter 1

Arise O Hero, Arise

'You are equal to Sugreeva in valour, and in wisdom, you are comparable to Rama and Lakshmana; You outshine everyone in strength, intelligence, vitality, and strength of character.'

'Your arms possess as much strength and power as the wings of the great Garuda—king of the birds'

'Arise, O Hanuman, and leap across this mighty ocean. Quell the anxiety and worry of the Vanara army and display your valour!'

As Jambavan continued to speak, each word was like a divine spark igniting the latent fires within the Rudra avatar.

With each utterance, Vayuputra's stature grew immensely, his form expanding beyond mortal limits. Chanting the sacred mantra—Jai Shri Ram—his size became colossal, his radiance eclipsing the very sun, casting a divine glow upon the awe-struck faces of the Vanara army.

In that moment, the curse that veiled his memory lifted, and all the celestial blessings once showered upon him as a child were rekindled in a blazing aura of glory. Hanuman stood among the Vanaras, not just as another Vanara warrior but as a spark of Mahadev Himself!

The Vanaras, gathered in throngs, gazed up in wonder and reverence at the magnificent spectacle. His presence was like that of the sun, a force of nature that none had ever witnessed. The sagacious and humble Maruti, now revealed the boundless power concealed within.

The son of the Wind God, the Rudra Avatara, Shiva Himself in the guise of a Vanara, proclaimed with divine authority: 'I claim my descent from the great Vayu. What to speak of leaping across this ocean, I can go as far as the sun, moon, and the planets. I can circle around the great Garuda a thousand times. If I want, I can snatch nectar even from the hands of Vajra-wielding Indra and the creator Brahma. I can uproot the entire island of Lanka and bring it back with me if needed. Cheer up O Vanaras, rest your worries.'

These were not the words of pride but of unshakeable confidence, meant to inspire and assure his comrades. Shri Hanuman's speech was a thunderous declaration of his capabilities, each word a testament to his dedication and service to Bhagavan Shri Rama.

As the Vanaras listened, their spirits were lifted from the depths of despair to the heights of hopeful anticipation. No hint of arrogance tainted Hanuman's declarations; his immense power was but a tool in the service of his master and his people.

Celebrating the boundless humility and selflessness of Hanuman, the Vanaras cheered, their voices echoing across the landscape, *Shri Ramadoot Hanuman kee jai*!

With the army's morale restored and their faith rekindled, Hanuman sought guidance from Jambavan.

'Tell me, O Jambavan, what should I do? Should I annihilate the entire Rakshasha army, kill Ravana, and rescue the venerable Sita? O Vanaras, you may begin celebrations, for it is my firm belief that I will locate the pious daughter of King Janaka.'

As the Vanaras erupted in joyous acclaim, Angad advised caution, suggesting that Hanuman return after locating Devi Sita, leaving further actions for Shri Rama's counsel.

Blessings flowed from Jambavan as he spoke of their eager anticipation for Hanuman's triumphant return. They would wait, he declared, immersed in prayer and divine invocations for his success.

Obedient to the commands of his leaders, Hanuman ascended the peak of the Mahendra mountain.

He offered His respects to Surya, Indra, Varuna, and Brahma. Facing the east, Hanuman bowed down to his father Vayu, and then, he turned southward, poised to make the historic leap across the formidable expanse of the ocean.

Key Takeaway
Lessons in Humility

One of the most significant things we can pick from Shri Ramadoot's character and life is how genuine humility always attracts blessings.

Humility is not making yourself small or believing yourself to be less. Rather, not making another person feel less because of who we are and what we do can constitute a wonderful aspect of a grounded individual.

Hanuman's personality was such that he never made someone else feel small. Moreover, his focus on serving a higher cause is driven to bring happiness to others—and such an attitude only evokes blessings from everyone.

When Shri Vayuputra grows in size and starts speaking about his divine abilities, he is not being haughty or boastful. As we move ahead in the book, Hanuman will walk the talk and demonstrate his divine abilities.

Self-deprecation disguised as humility can often come in the way of performing our duties. It can also be a ruse to skip working. Hanuman teaches us confidence to embrace our gifts—big or small. What matters is how we put our abilities to use. And if we sincerely attempt to do our best with our abilities, God's blessings in our life can make even the impossible easily possible.

Your Reflection

What do you feel constitutes humility?

Do you feel one can combine self-confidence and assurance with humility?

अंगद के संग लेन गए सिय,
खोज कपीस यह बैन उचारो।
जीवत ना बचिहौ हम सो जु,
बिना सुधि लाये इहाँ पगु धारो।
हेरी थके तट सिन्धु सबै तब,
लाए सिया-सुधि प्राण उबारो॥

'You went with Angad to fetch the information about Sita. Angad declared all of them would perish if none could find her whereabouts. When everyone became dead tired, you brought Sita's information and saved the life of the army.

Who in the world does not know your name to be *Sankat Mochan*— remover of troubles.'

(Sankatmochan Hanumanastak by Goswami Tulsidas)

Chapter 2

Overcoming Distractions

Shri Hanuman squatted down to prepare himself to leap from the peak of Mahendra mountain. Mahavir Hanuman pressed his feet on the mountain with such force that trees shed all their fragrant flowers. As the blossoms scattered on the ground, it appeared as if the entire area was carpeted with flowers.

The mighty son of Vayu then surged upward. The sheer power of his leap caused the meditating sages nearby to levitate, and animals scurried in disarray. Behind Hanuman, trees, shrubs, and flowers were caught up in the tumultuous wake of his ascent, painting a surreal backdrop to this extraordinary spectacle.

The Vanaras, witnessing this from afar, were awestruck. Their eyes wide, they beheld the majestic flight of Shri Ramadoot, their hearts swelling with pride and wonder at the flurry of nature trailing him.

Empowered by the sacred invocation of his beloved Lord Rama's name—a mantra potent enough to liberate souls from the cycles of birth and death—Hanuman felt a surge of indomitable confidence. This daunting leap across 1,200 kilometres was but a minor stride in his service for Shri Rama.

As Vayuputra soared across the vast ocean, he thought of how he would reassure Devi Sita upon locating her. And if any Rakshasa tried impeding his mission, they would meet their end.

He had already started visualising meeting and greeting his Lord with the news of locating Devi Sita.

The celestial beings, recognising the gravity of Shri Hanuman's quest, showered him with heavenly blossoms as the glorious son of Vayu cleaved through the skies. This cascade of flowers from the heavens mirrored the outpouring of support for the end of Ravana's tyrannical reign.

Ravana had been a menace for entire creation. To deliver all creatures from the clutches of pain and suffering, Bhagavan Shri Narayan had appeared in a human form as Shri Ramachandra.

The ocean god, Varuna observed the son of Vayu flying over him. Varun Dev wondered how he could be of assistance and service to the great Maruti. Varun Dev summoned a mountain named Mainak that had gained shelter in the ocean, fearing Indra's wrath.

It is said that once upon a time, mountains had wings. The mountains used to fly from one place to another, causing great anxiety and fear among the living creatures on Earth. Indra, being moved by the plight of the earthly beings, decided to chop off the wings of the mountains and render them stationary. Mainak took shelter of Varun Dev and was spared. He also served as an obstacle for the nefarious nether world beings from entering the earthly realm.

Varun Dev thought that Hanuman was on such an arduous journey that it would only be appropriate that he gets a bit of rest. In the past, it had been one of Shri Rama's ancestors, called Sagara, who had helped manifest the ocean for earthly beings. Varun Dev wanted to repay the debt of gratitude and also contribute to the divine mission of Lord Rama and Hanuman.

Handing the memo to Mainak, Varun Dev asked him to expand his size and offer his surface as a resting place for Shri Hanuman. As Hanuman saw Mainak expanding his form and size in front of him, he was momentarily taken back.

What was this colossal object carrying a golden hue trying to block his movement?

Before Lord Hanuman could smash the obstacle away from his path, Mainak appeared in a human-like form and revealed the purpose of his sudden appearance.

Mainak also revealed that Hanuman's father had previously helped Mainak when he was trying to escape Indra's punishment. Mainak offered his services of rest, food and rejuvenating beverages to Vayuputra.

The ever gracious Maruti listened to Mainak's heartfelt offer. With unwavering focus, he gently touched the peak of Mainak with his right hand, as a gesture of respect and acceptance of the mountain's service.

Vayuputra spoke soothing and gentle words to Mainak, 'Your kind intentions and the honour of your words itself have rejuvenated my spirit. However, the urgency of my mission allows no pause.' With these words, Hanuman soared onwards, his resolve as firm as ever.

The encounter with Mainak was but the first of the celestial tests laid before him, each designed to measure the depth of his intelligence, strength and devotion. As Shri Ramadoot continued his journey, the gods watched, ready to present the next divine challenge.

Key Takeaway
Perseverance Pays

For ordinary mortals like us, rest is compulsory. We cannot mindlessly imitate powerful personalities like Shri Hanuman. But the zeal, the focus, the purpose with which Lord Hanuman was moving towards his goal is something we all can take inspiration from.

I think of the successful people I know around me (not including public personalities), and I observe a theme. I am talking of the academically meritorious friends who have worked extremely hard to crack competitive exams, the spiritual seekers who have given up various comforts and distractions, the parents who have to raise a child, and so on.

Each successful human I know has had to resist the temptation of comfort and rest on their path to success. There is no sugarcoating the fact that detachment to comforts and attachment to the attainment of the goal precipitates success. The ones who fail to do so often languish in regret or sadly complain.

It is important to note that Lord Hanuman does not reject the idea of comfort, good food, and rest.

It turns out that a bit of discomfort is advantageous in learning something. In Adam Grant's amazing book, *Hidden Potential:*

The Science of Achieving Greater Things, he quotes research-backed evidence to show that being a little uncomfortable during the process of learning helps us to grow.

Cheating is easy; commitment to relationship needs work.
Oversleeping is easy; time management needs work.
Snacking is easy; maintaining a diet needs work.
Being a couch potato is easy; having a fitness regime needs work.
Splurging is easy; investing and saving up needs work.

But the joy, the relief, and euphoria accompanying the successful attainment of a positive goal or dream is ineffable. And so, let us pray to Lord Hanuman to bless us with a laser sharp focus to resist temptations, and work sincerely and confidently towards our goals.

You would have also noticed how Shri Ramadoot uses the power of visualisation, made extremely popular by teachers of the law of attraction. Significantly, Shri Ramadoot didn't just sit to visualise his goal but was taking action towards the attainment of the goal—that is the key to a successful manifestation.

Your Reflection

Think of the success that you have attained in your life journey. What were the ingredients that comprised that success?

Is there a goal you wish to work for or are already working on?

What temptations or distractions can you cut down to help in swifter realisation of that goal?

'हनूमान तेहि परसा कर पुनि कीन्ह प्रनाम । राम काजु कीन्हें बिनु मोहि कहाँ बिश्राम ॥'

Touching the mountain with his hand and offering *Pranam*, Hanuman said, 'Before completing Shri Rama's mission, there is no rest for me.'

Chapter 3

A Test of Merit and Intelligence

Albert Einstein once pondered the question: 'Is the universe a friendly place?'

This query resonates deeply when we reflect on our story. As Maruti soared towards Lanka, every celestial being and deity rejoiced, sensing the imminent downfall of Ravana and the liberation from his tyranny.

The devatas prepared a test for Hanuman. Why would a benevolent universe that supports and blesses our endeavours present such challenges?

Let us ponder this as we accompany Lord Hanuman on his journey.

The loving and friendly obstacle that came Hanuman's way in the form of Mainak was dealt with respect. Yet, as he continued moving forward, a new, daunting figure emerged.

Surasa, the mother of the Nagas and a formidable snake goddess, appeared in a fearsome guise to test Shri Ramadoot.

Indra, the king of the heavens, was in awe of Hanuman's strength and resolve but sought to test his intellect. Indra knew that mere physical prowess would not suffice for Hanuman's mission to find Devi Sita in Lanka. Indeed, success in life requires not only strength but also intelligence, character, and humility—qualities embodied by Shri Hanuman. Through this trial, Indra aimed to highlight Hanuman's sagacity.

At Indra's behest, Surasa blocked Hanuman's path, declaring that she had been ordained by the creator Brahma to consume any being who attempted to pass her. In response, Hanuman, with utmost humility, requested a postponement of his fate until after he completed his mission for Shri Rama.

Unyielding, Surasa insisted that Hanuman must enter her mouth, as decreed. As she enlarged her jaws in an attempt to devour him, Vayuputra expanded his form to match her scale. This contest of expansions continued until Surasa's mouth seemed large enough to swallow the heavens.

At that critical moment, Shri Ramadoot cleverly shrank to the size of a thumb, darted in and out of her gaping mouth, and reappeared before her, bowing in respect, assuming the *Anjali mudra*.

He declared, 'I have honoured Shri Brahma's blessing by entering your mouth, O Mother. Now, please grant me passage to Lanka to complete my quest for locating Devi Sita.'

Impressed by Shri Hanuman's wit and humility, Surasa resumed her divine form and blessed him, acknowledging her role in testing him and said that a person of Hanuman's qualities would be successful in every endeavour that he undertakes.

Thus, Vayuputra resumed his flight, overcoming two significant challenges. However, the path of ascension in life often attracts forces that seek to pull us down.

Key Takeaway
Success: Winning it and Keeping it

Hanuman was acting not just to unite Lord Rama and Devi Sita but his mission would eventually also lead to emancipation of the gods. And here they are posing a test.

Shouldn't the devatas actively aid Hanuman rather than posing such challenges?

Wasn't the journey from the Kishkinda (kingdom of Vanaras) to the southern shores arduous and challenging enough?

Success is not just in the attainment of a goal. True measure of success is how someone handles themselves and their success once they attain it.

So often we find people going astray from the values that brought them success once they reach their goal. Reaching a goal may be tough, but maintaining that success, that achievement is harder.

We find innumerable examples of public personalities who appeared in the public eye through the merit of talent and ability. But because they lacked in character, they could never justify their talent.

Ability and talent may lead you to the summit of success, but maintaining it requires strength of character, adaptability, calm temperament, and, importantly, intelligence.

It was abundantly clear Lord Hanuman was extremely capable. He had the ability, the power, the blessings. What the universal forces wanted to test was whether he had the right temperament and wisdom to find a way out if he or his mission hits a snag?

Entering Lanka would not just be about 'Hulk-smashing' through everything. Shri Hanuman would need to employ his wits, wisdom and intelligence to locate and deliver his message to Sita.

Maruti was carrying tremendous blessings with him. However, he meets a Naga lady who herself was carrying a blessing that none could pass over her.

Brute strength isn't always the answer, obviously.

Competitiveness also is not something that will always put you ahead in life.

What we learn from Shri Hanuman is that often, one has to let go of the ego, shrink the size of our pride, and act consciously according to the situation.

Hanuman could have kept up the act of increasing the size of His body in proportion to Surasa's gaping mouth, ready to devour him. But to keep outdoing her and engaging in a battle of displaying superiority would have meant wasting precious time. And thus, in an act of profound wisdom, and most importantly, humility, he shrunk his bodily size and found a way to win over Surasa.

And here is the secret of maintaining success: adaptability, willingness to put aside the ego if needed, and humility in acknowledging a roadblock and finding a way around it.

A person who has these characteristics, or works upon developing them, will find a way around any roadblock, and keep inventing themselves for success.

Take the example of personalities like Amitabh Bachchan and Sachin Tendulkar.

Mr Bachchan, one of Indian cinema's superstars, was almost bankrupt at one point in time. He had seen a failed business and political career. He agreed to host *Kaun Banega Crorepati*, accepted supporting actor roles, and adapted himself to the reality of his time. He hasn't looked back since.

The legendary Sachin had an illustrious career spanning decades. During this extraordinarily long career, Sachin adapted his game on numerous occasions to suit the team and ended up playing under the leadership of cricketers who had half his experience. Never did Sachin create an issue or bother for the rest of the team. He kept adapting, working towards the goal of playing for his nation, and moving forward.

So, if you have hit a roadblock in your pursuit towards a cherished goal, take a moment to remind yourself that the universe has your back and even challenges and obstacles prepare you for eventual success. Roadblocks make success even more gratifying. To conclude, I'd quote two different book titles of Ryan Holiday: *Ego is the Enemy* and *The Obstacle is the Way*.

Your Reflection

Think of a time when you faced a significant obstacle on your journey towards a goal. How did you initially approach the challenge? What lessons can you take from Shri Hanuman's encounter with Surasa to refine your approach to challenges in your own life?

राम काजु सबु करिहहु तुम्ह बल बुद्धि निधान। आसिष देइ गई सो हरषि चलेउ हनुमान।।

You will accomplish all the tasks of Shri Rama, O reservoir of strength and intelligence. Being blessed thus by Surasa, Hanuman happily moved forward.

Chapter 4

Dealing with Negativity

As the valorous son of Vayu flew with purpose towards his goal of reaching Lanka, he suddenly found his flight halted.

No matter how hard Pavanputra tried to move his limbs, he remained frozen. Then suddenly he found himself being pulled down with great force towards the ocean. As Hanuman was hurtling down towards the great ocean, he confronted the formidable sea monster, Simhika.

Known for her ability to ensnare her victims by seizing their shadows, Simhika saw in Hanuman's colossal form a feast that could quell her hunger for days. But Hanuman, undeterred by the imminent threat, prepared to face the monster head-on as he recalled how Sugreeva had warned him about the existence of such a creature living in the ocean.

With unwavering faith in his beloved Lord Shri Rama, the supremely intelligent Maruti fearlessly entered Simhika's mouth, assuming a tiny form. The devotion and the might of Vayuputra were such that he shattered through the inner organs of the demoness, emerging unscathed.

Witnessing Hanuman's triumph, the devatas collectively

exhaled a sigh of relief, their faith in the prowess of Hanuman reaffirmed. They marvelled at the display of his strength and wisdom. Acknowledging his status as a true hero, the devatas pronounced: 'A person who possesses the four virtues of patience, wisdom, intelligence, and skill can never fail in their undertaking.'

Our hero was now almost at the shores of Lanka.

Key Takeaway
Overcome Thoughts that Pull You Down

In a funny line from a popular Hindi film called *3 Idiots*, one of the characters says, *'Hum fail ho jaayein toh dukh hota hai par dost pass ho jaaye aur hum fail ho jaayein toh bohot zyada dukh hota hai.'*

This may be funny in the context of a movie. Still, it also paints a sorry picture of how human beings, despite eons of evolutionary process and material advancement, have not managed to ditch the conditionings of the reptilian brain.

In simpler words, quite a number of human beings believe, if not consciously, that another's flight of success means they will have less. Our happiness cannot be determined by who has less or more. If it is, then we are far away from happiness and contentment.

A human of healthy mind and consciousness would delight or at most, be indifferent to another's success and rise.

A healthy mind would treat another's rise as a potential, as an inspiration towards success and well-being.

It is one thing to be envious of another's rise and quite another to act on that envy. A sinister mind would not just be slighted by another's growth and rise but also try to pull him down.

We all would have been witness to this. If not personally, we'd have observed it in someone else's case—whether in the case of successful people needlessly facing trolling in the virtual world or office politics or sometimes even within family and relatives.

In the real world, there are not many Jambavans who can inspire one to attain greatness. More importantly, in our world, there aren't many like the Vanaras who would actively cheer and support our rise.

And far too often in our life journey, we may have to encounter someone like Simhika who will try and pull us down.

What should be the most appropriate response in such a situation?

We cannot control how another chooses to live their life; at best, we can hope and pray that if we work on our personal conduct and live a conscious life, others may be inspired and influenced to do so as well.

But we also need practical tips to counter the negativity that often can accompany growth. Let me enunciate a few tips that I have picked from Ramayana and Ramadoot's epic journey.

Be Prepared
There will be doubters; they may hate you for no reason, and, of course, some will actively cause discomfort. If we try to decode why someone does what they do, we will remain stuck forever. Instead, accept it as part of the package. Lord Hanuman did not resist falling down as Sugreeva had told him such a sea monster exists.

There will be people who despise other people's success. However, merely being aware of this sad reality is not enough.

Strengthen Your Inner Self
How to do that?
Well, believe in something bigger than just your ability and prowess. If there is anything that can induce awe or wonder, then allow that to act as a shield against negativity. Lord Hanuman had full faith in his mission, ability, and the power of remembrance of his beloved deity's name. He invokes that power of awe and reverence anytime we find Him stuck on his mission. And for the agnostics, we now also have some experimental data to back it up.

Dacher Keltner, author of the book *Awe*, Professor at University of California, Berkley, and founder of Greater Good Science Center, has studied the concept of awe for over 15 years. Keltner's research, which he has conducted with thousands of people worldwide, reveals the impact awe has on boosting vitality, reducing stress, and enhancing our overall levels of well-being.

Shri Hanuman could not remain despondent for long as he carried forever in his heart the reverence, the faith, and the awe induced by his love for Rama.

Maybe we can find awe and wonder in a deity like Lord Hanuman. But we can also find awe in nature, in a book, in an object, in a fellow human being, or simply in what we term as the universe. What is essential is that the feeling of awe and reverence should be a constant practice, and that will induce unshakeable belief and confidence in not just our ability but also ultimate success.

Block It Out
We saw how Lord Hanuman deals with negativity in this chapter. We can pick up a few things from him.

He does not waste his time trying to reason with Simhika. There is no dialogue or conversation, unlike the previous two obstacles or tests. He simply overcomes the negativity with faith in the name of his beloved Lord. Similarly, in our life's journey, there will be people who just cannot be reasoned with. If we waste our time trying to reason with them, we will only end up frustrated.

Instead, anytime in life when you find yourself being pulled down by another's negativity, remind yourself of the larger goal and purpose of your life and keep moving forward like our hero, Hanuman. Sometimes, what pulls us down are our own thoughts, and self-doubts. For many, their greatest adversary, sadly, is their own thought process. That is the kind of negativity that needs to be quelled immediately. It is how the brain coach Jim Kwik says: kill those A.N.T.S or automatic negative thoughts. These ANTS are our Simhika. Quell them and rise above and beyond.

Your Reflection
Think of a time when you felt pulled down—whether by external negativity (jealousy, criticism, or opposition) or internal doubts. How did you respond? Did you try to reason with the negativity, or did you rise above it like Shri Hanuman?

महाबीर बिक्रम बजरंगी ।
कुमति निवार सुमति के संगी ॥

You are a great hero, valiant and with a body as strong as a thunderbolt. You dispel negative thoughts and are a companion of wisdom and good sense.

Section 3
Do Not Lose Hope

Chapter 1

Power of Association

Ravana's Lanka, a golden city, was perched majestically on the peaks of the Trikuta mountains. As Hanuman landed on the shores of the island, he was struck with awe at the truly breathtaking sight of the golden city, its glory reflecting in the setting sun.

Stretching as far as Lord Hanuman's eyes could see, Lanka was fortified with such impenetrable strength that it seemed like an insurmountable obstacle for the Vanara army to breach.

Undeterred, the wise son of Vayu, Shri Hanuman gathered his wits, and became mindful of the present moment. But realising that worrying about the future was a futile exercise, he proceeded ahead, his determination unwavering, chanting the auspicious name of Shri Rama.

As the sun dipped below the horizon and the full moon painted the sky with its silvery glow, Hanuman, with his divine yogic power, had shrunk his formidable form to the size of a tiny kitten. Stealthily, he approached the imposing gates of Lanka, a city that appeared as impregnable as it was magnificent.

However, as he was looking to sneak in, he got into a bit of 'immigration trouble'.

Lankini, the guardian of Lanka, with her towering presence and fierce eyes, knocked Maruti back and demanded sternly, 'Who dares enter the realms of Lanka uninvited?'

Despite the unwelcome confrontation and being struck unprovoked, Shri Vayuputra kept his identity hidden. Annoyed at this unexpected obstacle and invigorated by a surge of righteous indignation, he struck back at Lankini, using only half his strength. Yet, even this restrained blow was potent enough to send the guardian crashing to the ground.

That punch by Shri Ramadoot led to a 'mentos moment' for the guardian of Lanka.

Lankini lay dazed for a moment before a profound realisation dawned upon her. As she slowly rose, her demeanour changed from hostility to reverence. She bowed reverentially before Lord Hanuman, saying 'O divine emissary, your strike has awakened me to a prophecy long foretold by the creator, Brahma, himself!'

Lankini had been a resident of Brahma-*loka* where she had been granted the position of a security guard. However, perturbed by her haughty and egoistic behaviour, Brahma had condemned her to fall down and assume the position for the evil Ravana.

However, when Brahma noticed her repentant mindset, He assured her that once she has had sufficient time to reflect, one day, upon being punched by a Vanara, she would be freed from her exile and be able to return back home.

'Lord Brahma had not only forewarned the punch, he had also predicted that your arrival would herald the downfall of Lanka's tyrant, Ravana, and the restoration of righteousness,' she explained, her voice a mixture of awe and relief.

With these revelations, Lankini not only granted Lord Hanuman access to Lanka but also imparted blessings for his forthcoming endeavours.

With Lankini's blessings, Maruti ventured forth into the city, his spirit buoyed by the divine affirmation of his purpose, chanting the holy name of Lord Rama, ready to face the challenges that lay ahead in the heart of Ravana's empire.

Key Takeaway
The Joys of Satsang

To add context to Lankini's fall from a heavenly realm, according to Vedic understanding, there are different levels within heavenly planets, just as there are various levels of hellish planets. Depending on the type of karma one accrues over the course of a lifetime, a soul is granted entry into either heaven or hell.

Brahma-*loka* is the highest level of heavenly abode a soul can access. But one can fall down even from that level of ascendence as it happened with Lankini. Even Bhagavan Shri Krishna points out something similar in the Bhagavad Gita:

आब्रह्मभुवनाल्लोकाः पुनरावर्तिनोऽर्जुन (8:16)

Beyond the heavenly realms are the spiritual planets and the abodes of Bhagavan Shiva and Bhagavan Vishnu. The abodes of Hari (Narayana) and Hara (Shiva) are eternal, and for one to attain these, a soul has to overcome the bonds of karma.

Additionally, Goswami Tulsidas, author of *Ramcharitmanas* derives an incredibly potent and wonderful lesson from this incident, and I wish to elaborate upon it.

'तात स्वर्ग अपबर्ग सुख धरिअ तुला एक अंग । तूल न ताहि सकल मिलि जो सुख लव सतसंग ॥'

Shri Tulsidas uses the encounter of Lord Hanuman and Lankini to highlight the glory of *satsang*, or positive, saintly association.

Poetically, Tulsi Baba points out how even a moment's association with a saintly person like Hanuman (even though it had to arrive in the form of a punch, ouch!) led Lankini back to her original home and heavenly abode.

Tulsidas says *all heavenly pleasures and even liberation cannot compare to the joy of even a moment's association with saintly people.*

Satsang—the derived meaning of the Sanskritam word can mean association with that which is true, right, good, and auspicious. And this word *satsang*, does not only imply saintly association or something profoundly spiritual. *Satsang* can also be found around friends and family, even popular culture, or even inanimate objects.

In my personal journey, I have derived a lot of learning from pop culture icons like Snoopy, TV shows like *Ted Lasso*, or even from fictional books and characters.

Additionally, when I reflect back upon my life, the most memorable, joyous, uplifting moments have come when I am around my most cherished loved ones. So I am completely affirmative to the idea that there is no greater joy than good company as Tulsidas points out.

Of course, it is not only joy that is induced through good company or *satsang*. *Satsang* enables one to learn critical life lessons, grow as a human being, and be led towards spiritual upliftment.

On the contrary, *Dush-sang* (or bad company) leads one to misery, defeat and fall in life. Take for instance Duryodhana and the Pandavas in Mahabharat—the classic case study on the power of association.

Duryodhana was surrounded by people with a negative mindset like his uncle Shakuni, brother Dusshashana and friend Karna. All they ever did was to support and fuel hate and anger towards the Pandavas.

Contrary to Duryodhana, the Pandavas had the blessing and wise company of sages, and of course, the love of Yogeswarishar, Parameshwar Bhagavan Shri Krishna, which kept them afloat amidst all the troubles they went through in life.

Even in the Ramayana, we see how the sagely company of Shri Hanuman led Sugreeva to regain his lost power, kingdom and spouse. It was Shri Hanuman who connected Sugreeva to Shri Rama and Lakshmana, and he was the one who had advised Sugreeva to forge a bond of friendship with Shri Rama.

Vali, Sugreeva's brother had not just taken away his kingdom but had also kept his spouse captive, and killed their child as well. For the same reason, we see why Rama also chooses to align with Sugreeva despite him not being as strong as Vali. Lord Rama felt that to align with someone who himself was an abductor of another's wife for his needs would be hypocritical.

Choosing who we spend our time with, and who we associate with is like choosing our destiny. One life coach from America, late Jim Rohn used to say:

'You are the average of five people you spend most time with.'

If we surround ourselves with people who are driven, optimistic, encouraging, and kind, we will eventually develop such kinds of attitudes towards life. If not, the mind can easily descend into negative states.

And especially when it comes to our spiritual lives, one moment's association with a powerful spiritual person or resource has the power and potential to completely transform our life for the better.

If I were to give my personal example, this book that I am getting to write and present to you and every big or small win for me in my life stems from the impact of a few lines that I ended up reading from the *Bhagavad Gita As It Is* by Swami Prabhupada when I was a sixteen-year-old boy.

P.S. I didn't just restrict myself to reading a few lines. I read the entire book and since then continue to delve into the divine literature.

Your Reflection

Before we proceed further, I implore you to reflect upon a few things:

- Who are those *five* people you spend the most time with?
- Who has been the most uplifting association in your life?
- Think of the books, movies or shows that have had the most uplifting impact on you. Make a list and keep them handy in case you need a pick-me-up.
- Last, how can you be a *'satsang'* yourself for the people in your life?

Chapter 2

Hanuman
The Saviour of Gods

The beauty and glory of the great scripture of Ramayana is that we find additions, minor variances, and adaptations according to different traditions and cultures. Such tales reflect the rich and unique tapestry of oral storytelling in Sanatana Dharma.

I share this chapter as an offering for the devotees of Lord Hanuman, who are inspired to worship him. Even if you are not spiritually or devotionally inclined, this short chapter can be a fun read.

Legends and folklore suggest that even before Hanuman met Lankini, he had to face two immensely powerful and significant personalities, Kalapurush and Shani Dev.

Crossing over the ocean, obstacles, distractions, and tests, Hanuman finally landed on the island of Lanka. Before Vayuputra could even catch a breath, he was kicked with brute strength sending him reeling back. The mighty Hanuman recovered quickly and was shocked to see Kalapurush, god of death, standing in front of him!

Kalapurush was taken aback on seeing the Rudra avatar, Lord Hanuman, and felt sorry for kicking him.

Ravana had stationed the shackled Kalapurush strategically on the island so that anyone who was looking to enter Lanka would first have to meet death!

Hanuman, the embodiment of Lord Shiva, transcended the limitations of time and death. As Kalapurush, bound by Ravana's misuse of power, shared his plight, Lord Hanuman's compassion was stirred. He released Kalapurush from his shackles, a testament to his divine power and mercy.

Kalapurush blessed Shri Hanuman, promising that anyone who sincerely worshipped him would be granted the divine gift of immunity to the fear of death, a profound and powerful blessing.

Next up, Lord Hanuman heard the wails and moans of someone who felt like he was in a lot of pain. As the compassionate Maruti followed the anguished cries, he discovered a person in distress, bound and hanging upside down in a small cave. With a swift and compassionate act, Maruti freed the person from his suffering, filling the air with a sense of relief and gratitude.

This person was none other than the feared planet *Shani* (Saturn).

Those who are familiar with astrology know how Shani is equally feared and revered. A *dasha*, or a period of time when a person is being influenced by the gaze of Saturn, is said to be really challenging. And there is no fool-proof way of appeasing Shani either. Shani is said to be a cold, apathetic, but a just personality. He has no use of appeasement; his task is to mete out justice. However, knowledgeable astrologers say that for humans who have accumulated good/pious karma, *Shani dasha* can be extremely favourable.

Ravana, who was said to be an expert on astrology, bound up Shani and ensured that the feared gaze of Shani did not befall anyone in Lanka, least of all the king.

Overwhelmed with gratitude, Shani Dev bestowed his blessings upon Shri Hanuman for his emancipation. Shani pronounced that any person who sincerely and devotedly worships Hanuman would be spared the wrath of Shani's gaze.

Key Takeaway
Hanuman Drives Away Obstacles
It is the experience of the author, expert astrologers, and so many sincere spiritual practitioners that worshipping Hanuman with sincerity, and most importantly, learning and applying lessons from his life leads one to be free from anxiety, problems and obstacles. One develops faith in the benevolence of the universe and in the self as well.

So anytime in life when you feel fearful, scared, beaten down, and miserable, read stories of Lord Hanuman, chant the name of his beloved Shri Rama, and read *Hanuman Chalisa* while surrendering your worries to the divine Maruti.

May you always be blessed with success and joy.

Your Reflection
What are the shackles that hold you back?

संकट हरे मिटै सब पीरा ।
जो सुमिरै हनुमत बल बीरा ॥

Problems disappear and miseries are removed for those who meditate on the powerful Shri Hanuman.

Chapter 3

Stealth Mode Activated

The venerable author of *Ramacharitmanas*, Goswami Tulsidas penned a beautiful *chaupai* or verse as Hanuman enters Lanka. This verse, when chanted and remembered, is believed to invoke auspiciousness and good luck.

Whether you're an interested reader or *a spiritual scientist,* you can try this practice in various situations. It could be before a journey, an interview, an exam, or any significant event in your life.

प्रबिसि नगर कीजे सब काजा । हृदयँ राखि कोसलपुर राजा ॥

'Remembering the lord of Ayodhya (Shri Rama) in your heart, enter the city and complete all the tasks.'

By maintaining a positive intention and sincerely remembering God, we can forge a personal connection that leads us to an assured victory.

Also, when one sets out on a mission that is truly selfless and aimed at bringing delight and harmony for all, even adversaries end up blessing you as it happened for Lord Hanuman with Lankini blessing him before she left.

The astute Anjaneya, mindful of the importance of secrecy, chose to make his entry at the onset of dusk. His aim was to infiltrate unnoticed, locate Devi Sita, and deliver Lord Rama's message without a hint of his presence.

Valmiki Muni's words paint a picture of the awe-inspiring beauty of Lanka as Lord Hanuman enters the city on the night of the full moon. The well laid-out paths and roads, adorned with bright flowers, seemed to guide his way. The archways, bedecked with gems, sparkled in the moonlight, a testament to the opulence of the city.

Lord Hanuman's ears were filled with the sounds of joy and laughter emanating from the city's houses, intermingled with the melodious tunes of intricate musical instruments.

Maruti went house to house within the city, looking for Devi Sita. During his search, he came across various scenes in Lanka.

He witnessed various demons engaged in sensual acts with women who resembled celestial damsels.

He witnessed various spies and surveillance teams scanning each section of the city.

He noticed Lanka wasn't just about revelry and mirth; Yatudhanas, a group of rakshasas or demons were also engaged in chanting of mantras and prayers. They were engaged in spiritual practice by Ravana to ensure continued prosperity for him and his kingdom.

He noticed the might of Ravana's army and different classes of warriors that formed innumerable battalions.

Hanuman slowly made his way to the most luminous and grandiose structure in the city of gold—the palace of the Rakshasha king Ravana.

If the rest of the city was a testament to the divine craftsmanship of Vishwakarma, then Ravana's palace was a celestial marvel, a symphony of gold and jewels that seemed to defy the laws of space and time. Lord Hanuman, not one to be easily swayed by such opulence, focused on his mission and stealthily made his way inside.

As Maruti continued with his search, he came across the famed flying vehicle of Ravana called *Puspak Vimana*.

The evil king, Ravana had stolen the flying machine from his cousin Kubera, a devout worshipper of Ma Lakshmi. The machine, ironically, bore the insignia of the very deity the lusty king had affronted.

Lord Hanuman couldn't help but chuckle at Ravana's foolishness, his audacity to abduct the incarnation of the Devi of wealth and fortune in a machine that had her own insignia!

Moving deeper into the vast confines of Ravana's palace, Lord Hanuman entered the realm of the demon king's harem. Here, Ravana kept countless women, many of whom had been forcefully taken from their homes, succumbing to his overwhelming power. The scene was chaotic: women lay scattered, intoxicated, their attire in disarray, some on the ground, others on their beds.

This environment presented a profound challenge for the eternally celibate Shri Hanuman. The divine soul who scarcely allowed his gaze to linger on a woman now found himself amidst a sea of them. Tasked with finding Devi Sita, he had no choice but to scrutinise each face thoroughly, despite the discomfort it brought him.

Yet, in this den of seduction, Hanuman's virtue remained untainted. The sight of these beautiful women, capable of beguiling even the wisest sages, did not sway his pure heart.

This episode reflects the types of trials we might face on our paths to success. Often, life places us in situations that starkly contrast with our values. Nonetheless, maintaining a composed and focused demeanour in carrying out our duties paves the way to success.

Continuing his search, Lord Hanuman determined that none of these women resembled the divine Sita. His journey led him next to a figure of immense power asleep on a royal bed—the formidable Ravana himself. In this first encounter, Lord Hanuman, rather than feeling revulsion or anger, was struck by Ravana's majestic presence.

It led Shri Hanuman to muse: *if only Ravana had cultivated his character as diligently as his power, he might have been a ruler of unmatched dominion across all realms.*

Such is the nature of the righteous: to see potential and goodness, even in those lost to darkness.

Shri Ramachandra, too, had harboured similar sentiments upon first facing Ravana, lamenting the demon king's lack of moral restraint before the inevitable clash.

Hanuman noted the battle scars adorning Ravana's formidable frame: marks from *Lord Narayana's Sudarshan Chakra, a scar from the tusk of Indra's elephant Airavata, and a wound from Indra's thunderbolt.*

Near Ravana's bed, among the sleeping women and scattered delicacies and fragrances, stood out a celestial-looking lady adorned in splendid jewellery.

For a brief moment, the great Maruti leapt up in joy and started kissing his tail! It seemed he had finally spotted Sita.

However, this feeling of elation was fleeting.

How could this lady be Ma Sita, wondered Shri Ramadoot?

How could Ma Sita sleep so soundly and peacefully away from her beloved?

Devi Sita wouldn't be enchanted by the celestials even if they tried. Her love and devotion to Rama was greater than anyone and anything else. This divine-looking lady (it was Ravana's queen, Mandodari) was not Sita, even though her physical attributes and divine appearance misled Maruti into believing she was.'

Vayuputra had crossed the mighty ocean, overcome various

obstacles, managed to sneak into an impenetrable Lanka but despite extensive search, he still had no clue of Sita's location. Slowly but surely, Maruti's mind started brimming with doubts and worry as he exited the palatial palace of Ravana.

What if the divine Vaidehi had given up her life in a state of hopelessness?

What if the devious demons had killed her on witnessing her resolute resistance?

Hanuman wondered, what would Sugreeva say if he returned without any conclusive evidence about Sita?

How would he show his face to his beloved Lord Rama?

Hanuman resolved that if he did not locate Devi Sita, he would fast until death. He couldn't bear to inform Lord Rama on his failure to locate Devi Sita. He had observed that only the hope of seeing Sita again was keeping Lord Rama alive. If Sita weren't found, then surely, Rama would perish, and that would, in turn, mean that the entire clan would perish, for such was their love for Sita and Rama.

Mahaveera Vajrangi was swamped with negative and despondent thoughts.

Did he overcome these thoughts?

Did some divine intervention occur yet again to guide the sage warrior?

As Maruti wrestled with his despair, we are left to ponder: how do we face seemingly insurmountable challenges in our own quests?

Key Takeaway
Don't Let Emotions Bog You Down

I thoroughly love this particular section of the Ramayana for one reason: Even a superhero like Lord Hanuman can be seeped with self-doubt and be prone to despondency!

Heck, our venerable hero was so grief-stricken that he contemplated suicide! To an uninformed mind, such things may make the deities ordinary, but for the intelligent and wise, these attributes and descriptions add to the divinity and create a bond of love and relatability to our deities and heroes.

Hey, we mortals can latch on to hope. It is okay; we are not broken; we are not pathetic to feel low, and bad when we feel there is no hope.

Ramayana, as divine literature, does not discourage us from embracing the emotions that make us human. Valmiki Muni's description of the emotional state of the central characters, who, by the way, are told to be of divine origins, is fascinating.

There is Lord Rama lamenting and almost losing his balance of mind after Devi Sita's abduction.

Lord Rama is overcome with grief on seeing Lakshmana knocked out by Indrajit in the battlefield.

Bharata's emotionally charged response on realising the conspiracy hatched by his own mother is also very relatable.

Here, we see Shri Hanuman being overcome by doubts and grief upon realising that he is unable to execute his mission.

The idealism of the Ramayana as a scripture does not make people into mechanical robots devoid of emotions, which are essentially the juice of life.

What the Ramayana teaches us is for us to be real and embrace each emotion fully; to not linger too long in a state of grief or despondency but move towards overcoming the feelings that bog us down.

We see that although Lord Rama was shattered about the abduction of his beloved, he regains his composure on being counselled by Lakshmana.

Despite the heartbreak of being separated from his adoring brother, Bharata chooses the path of duty and completes his task of handling the kingdom effectively.

Ma Kaushalya gracefully bears the pain of losing the company of her son and the death of her husband.

I can go on and on and list a number of examples of characters in the Ramayana who overcome pain and despondency not by denying it but by embracing the present situation and working their way out of it. Even when these characters are going through intense heartbreak and situations, they do not romanticise the despondency but choose to transform it.

The relatability that the scripture of Ramayana induces is what makes the tale timeless. All of us go through grief, doubt, worry, and anxieties. All of us seek shelter, hope, and upliftment. This is where *satsang* of stories like the one we're learning from matters tremendously.

As always, a conscious and active human will seek practical steps. You may ask, if it was easy for these luminaries to work through grief. We are not yet there. Can there be practical ways of embracing and yet retaining balance in the face of grief and uncertainty? Most definitely, yes.

Your Reflection

Think back on a time in your life when you felt so overwhelmed that you wanted to quit. This could have been due to a relationship, job, family situation, education or just about anything. This may be a bit difficult to process but do give it a shot.

मसक समान रूप कपि धरी । लंकहि चलेउ सुमिरि नरहरी ॥

You took a tiny form and entered Lanka remembering that Lord Hari was impersonating a human (Rama).

Chapter 4

Give Up, Giving

In a world where despair often leads one soul to succumb every forty seconds, the stories of our ancient scriptures like the Ramayana offer not just tales of yore but vital life lessons that resonate through time. The epic transcends the narrative of a prince in exile and his battle against a demon king to reveal profound truths about the human condition—truths that remain as relevant today as they were, millennia ago.

Amidst the saga, Hanuman's moment of despondency becomes a powerful lesson in resilience and hope. Confronted with overwhelming despair in his mission to find Devi Sita, Shri Hanuman contemplates abandoning his life and purpose.

However, it is here, in the depths of despair that he finds the strength through positive self-talk and prayer.

The mighty hero who leaped across the great ocean with ease reminds himself that giving in to negative thoughts was not ideal in any scenario. Giving up without trying more sincerely was not good. Despite the thorough search and scanning of the most secure locations in Lanka, it was possible, thought Ramadoot, that he may have overlooked some part of the gigantic city.

'Being enthusiastic and cheerful in our endeavours is the basis of abundance and joy. Enthusiastic engagement in activities is what eventually leads to success. Giving up life may seem to be a compelling option, but only a person who is alive can get another chance at success and victory.'

Giving himself this positive pep talk and providing us with a success mantra for life, the wise Maruti affirms to renew his search once again. He vows to keep looking for Devi Sita until he gets her *darshan*.

As soon as Lord Hanuman makes a determined vow in his mind, he spots a beautiful grove full of big, fruit-laden trees. The Ashoka Vatika was a heavily guarded thick forest grove surrounded by other small groves and thick foliage from all sides. Lord Hanuman realised he had wholly overlooked that entire stretch during his search. Before proceeding to the grove, Lord Hanuman takes the shelter of a heartfelt prayer and invokes divine blessings.

नमोऽस्तु रामाय सलक्ष्मणाय देव्यै **च** तस्यै जनकात्मजायै ।
नमोऽस्तु रुद्रेन्द्रयमानिलेभ्यो नमोऽस्तु चन्द्रार्कमरुद्गणेभ्यः ॥

'I offer my respects to Lakshmana, Rama and the divine daughter of Janaka. I offer salutations to Rudra, Indra, Yama and Vayu. Salutations to Sun, Moon and Maruts.'

The saints and devotees mention that the above verse can be used as a mantra to find lost things.

There is a bit of variation in the *Valmiki Ramayan* and *Ramcharitmanas* by Goswami Tulsidas on how Lord Hanuman finally locates Devi Sita.

Goswami Tulsidas' narrative is sweeter and aimed at invoking love for God. Let us delve into that before we proceed.

रामायुध अंकित गृह सोभा बरनि न जाइ । नव तुलसिका बृंद तहँ देखि हरष कपिराइ ॥

Hanuman's thorough search across the opulent city of Lanka reveals no sign of Devi Sita until a divinely distinct house catches his attention. Marked by the sacred syllables 'Ra' and 'Ma' and adorned with a flourishing Tulsi plant, it stands out as a beacon of devotion in a city devoted to sensory pleasures. Inside, chants in praise of Rama echo, revealing not a demon, but a saint in disguise.

'Who in Lanka could so boldly honour Lord Rama?' Hanuman wonders, intrigued by the chants of Rama's name emanating from within Lanka, a city where people worshipped only the body temple; a city where people were focussed only upon sense enjoyment, who would be rebellious enough to lead such a different lifestyle?

A little context for the reader here:

In Vedic Santana Dharma, especially in the Vaishnavism sect, chanting the names of God and worshipping (nurturing) the Tulsi plant is considered one of the paths to attaining love and grace of God.

This house belonged to no ordinary inhabitant but to Vibhishana, the virtuous brother of Ravana, who lived a life of spiritual defiance amid Lanka's decadence.

Disguised as an old sage, Shri Hanuman was warmly welcomed by Vibhishana, who sensed a divine presence.

Revealing his identity, Lord Hanuman shares the tale of Rama, uplifting Vibhishana's spirits. Tulsidas poetically captures Vibhishana's plight in Lanka as a tongue residing amidst sharp teeth—an existence amidst discord yet untouched by its peril.

On hearing the narration of Shri Rama *Katha* and with a brief association of Lord Hanuman, Vibhishana feels uplifted and blessed, almost as if he had the darshan of his beloved Shri Rama!

Goswami Tulsidas poetically describes Vibhishana's stay

in Lanka as the presence of the tongue that is housed between sharp teeth! Not only could Vibhishana relate with the people in Lanka, but he also had a dearth of good associations and like-minded people to share his thoughts and feelings with.

With gratitude at the divine orchestrated serendipity, Vibhishana directs Mahavir towards Devi Sita's captivity in the Ashoka Vatika.

Emboldened and discreet, Lord Hanuman ventures towards the grove, setting the stage for a historical encounter that has enchanted devotees since eons.

Key Takeaway
Believe in Yourself and in the Divine
At the beginning of the chapter, I have already mentioned the lesson from Lord Hanuman's journey until now is to not give in to the stream of negative thoughts and ideas. Shri Hanuman's words of self-affirmation should serve as an effective reminder to keep living, keep hoping, and keep trying even in the face of the most adverse situations.

Next, a highly significant lesson to be learned here is how Shri Ramadoot is not just dependent upon his efforts and prowess, but also makes it a point to offer prayers and seek blessings as he steps up efforts to begin his search again.

Often, so many of us remain stuck in either/or when it comes to choosing between spirituality and worldly engagements. Either a person is solely obsessed with action, or we find fatalistic people who only adopt prayer without any effort on their part. But it should not be so. At least that is not what is the essence of our epics like Ramayana and Mahabharata or what Shri Krishna teaches to Arjuna.

Holistic success is a combination of both sincere efforts and divine blessings.

As we see, even in the divine literature of Bhagavad Gita, Shri Krishna advises Arjuna to do his duty, which was to engage in ghastly but necessary warfare, but also constantly remember Him or Paramatma.

Lord Hanuman was arguably the most powerful and wise being of his age. He was supremely blessed with powers and prowess. Yet, we witness how he too is submerged in doubts.

One can have all the prowess in the world and still life situations may leave us feeling stumped.

Here is walks in *faith*.

Here in walks in the *power of prayers*.

Anyone who has even remotely been connected to an authentic spiritual practice will vouch for the healing, uplifting, and even miraculous powers of a sincere prayer. A sincere prayer, surrendering your worries, and seeking shelter and guidance can help the mind overcome even the most hopeless of situations.

Lord Hanuman, despite all his powers, prowess, and abilities, does not forget to seek blessings either before leaping across the mighty ocean or now as he is renewing his search.

It is divine inspiration that leads Maruti towards the Ashoka Grove to Sita. Or even if we consider the narration of Ramcharitmanas, it is divine inspiration that leads him towards Vibhishan's house.

A simple practice of lighting a lamp and chanting the names of God (like Shri Rama Jaya Rama Jaya Jaya Rama or any mantra of choice) can give immense mental fortitude and inner strength in the face of adversity. Continuing such simple practices even on the sunny days of our life can keep us humble and grounded in success as well. It does not take elaborate rituals, routines, and processes to establish a connection with God.

Your Reflection

Have you ever experienced the power of prayers? How can you inculcate a practice of yoga (union) with the Supreme spirit, a deity or God in your daily life along with your work and responsibilities?

अस मैं अधम सखा सुनु मोहू पर रघुबीर । कीन्ही कृपा सुमिरि गुन भरे बिलोचन नीर ॥

O Friend, listen! I am fallen and unworthy, yet the great Lord Raghubeer (Shri Rama) has showered His grace upon me. Remembering His divine virtues, my eyes fill with tears.

Section 4
Proceed with Sensitivity

Chapter 1

Inscrutable Destiny

As Shri Hanuman headed towards the Ashoka Grove, a renewed vigour replaced the despondency that had momentarily clouded his spirit.

The Ashoka Grove greeted him with its exquisite beauty—luxuriant gardens and ponds shimmering with crystalline clarity. Vayuputra marvelled at exotic fruits and blossoms, unlike any he had seen before.

Bathed in the ethereal light of the full moon, the grove's opulence seemed to rival, perhaps even surpass, that of the heavenly realms. As Maruti leaped gracefully from one tree to another, the animals and birds stirred, raining down fragrant petals on him.

Yet, as wondrous as the grove appeared, it harboured a peculiar silence—no male guards were present, only Rakshasis, their demonic eyes vigilant, encircling the grove. In his diminutive form, Lord Hanuman navigated stealthily, driven by his mission to locate Devi Sita.

Suddenly Hanuman's attention fell on what seemed like a golden tree. 'How can there be a tree made of gold!' he exclaimed.

On closer inspection, he realised it was a rosewood (*simshupa*) tree, its trunk aglow with the golden reflection from the platform below. Climbing higher for a better vantage point, a sorrowful wail reached his ears. Nearby, amidst hideous demonesses, sat a woman whose divine radiance seemed out of place in this dark setting.

She appeared like a fallen angel from the heavens. Her clothes were soiled, and it seemed she hadn't been eating well, for she looked emaciated. Surrounded by hideous and morbidly scary-looking demonesses, the grieving lady looked utterly out of place but divinely resplendent.

Dressed in yellow, her beauty transcended that of the damsels of the heavens, and her appearance was strikingly similar to his beloved Shri Rama. Hanuman knew within his heart for sure that this lady was none other than Sita.

The observant Lord Hanuman noticed that this divine woman, who seemed kind, gentle, and capable of being the mother of the entire existence was not wearing any jewellery.

Shri Hanuman recalled seeing someone like her months back when he was sitting alongside a few other Vanara leaders atop the Rishimukha mountains. On noticing the forest dwellers, the lady who was being abducted by a demon had thrown her ornaments down, hoping that these may be discovered as a clue by her loved ones in search of her. This divine lady's description also matched that which was described to him by Shri Rama before he left for the search.

A profound joy stirred in Lord Hanuman, intertwined with a piercing sorrow. Here was the daughter of Janaka, the consort of the heroic Rama, ensnared in unwarranted misery.

Strange are the ways of fate, he mused. Despite her nobility and grace, Devi Sita was compelled to endure the grotesque company of her captors.

Before the expedition, there had been murmurs among the Vanara army: Was it even worth putting in so much effort for a woman? The lifelong celibate, Shri Hanuman, too, couldn't really relate or understand why a Kshatriya hero like Rama grieved so intensely for a woman.

But on seeing Devi Sita, Hanuman felt each and every effort of Rama and the army was worth it to secure Sita. Shri Ramadoot felt the same level of devotion for Devi Sita as he had felt for Lord Rama.

Hanuman also felt a deep sense of remorse for his beloved Lord Shri Rama.

How had the Lord endured such separation, he asked. How had he sustained himself apart from his beloved Sita for even a moment?

Brought back to the present by Devi Sita's sobs, Maruti knew he must act wisely. He needed to offer her reassurance and convey Rama's message without drawing attention.

As Vayuputra meditated on his next move, the eastern sky began to blush with the first light of dawn. The silence of the early morning was broken by the melodic strains of expert musicians and the sonorous voices of bards extolling the glories of their king. Ravana, roused from his deep slumber by these adulations, stirred with thoughts swirling around Sita.

Still inebriated from the previous night's revelries, Ravana staggered to his feet, his mind a tumult of desire. Flanked by a retinue of enamoured damsels, he began his descent towards the Ashoka Grove. Despite his conquests that spanned the known worlds, the demon king found himself enslaved by an untamed heart, plotting vain words to charm the unyielding Devi Janaki.

From a vantage point among the lush foliage, Shri Ramadoot watched the approach of the lust-driven monarch. Concealed within the branches, his form barely stirring, he observed every movement, his mind as alert as ever.

The scene before him sharpened his resolve. Hanuman knew the weight of the task ahead and prepared to act with both wisdom and courage.

Key Takeaway
Learn To Pick Ourselves Up

The short lesson that I wish to draw your attention to here in this chapter is Shri Hanuman's renewed enthusiasm and eagerness to carry out his mission. As soon as he uses positive affirmations and prayers, he immediately springs back into action with a lot of determination.

I am reminded of a quote from my favourite movie series, *The Dark Knight Trilogy*. Bruce/Batman's father says:

'Why do we fall, Bruce? We fall so that we can learn to pick ourselves up.'

For me, one of the endearing aspects to life is how we get up after a fall, an impediment, or an obstacle. Being despondent can be a natural response to failure but conscious growth lies in tackling it with prayers and affirmations and getting back to work with renewed enthusiasm.

It is as Bhagvan Shri Krishna explains in the Bhagavad Gita:

सुखदुःखे समे कृत्वा लाभालाभौ जयाजयौ ।
ततो युद्धाय युज्यस्व नैवं पापमवाप्स्यसि ॥2.38॥

Without worrying about victory or defeat, gain or loss, you engage in your actions for that work itself becomes a tool for liberation.

And Lord Hanuman's example shows, such an attitude eventually leads to success as well.

Your Reflection

Think of a time when you felt disheartened or lost motivation in pursuit of a goal. What helped you regain your enthusiasm?

निज पद नयन दिएँ मन राम पद कमल लीन । परम दुखी भा पवनसुत देखि जानकी दीन ॥

Head down, absorbed in remembrance of her Rama, Vayuputra felt saddened looking at the grieving form of Ma Janaki.

Chapter 2
Resilience of the Warrior Princess

Shri Hanuman started his journey to search for Devi Sita as a minister of Sugreeva. It is verily the meeting with Sita that transformed Hanuman into Shri Ramadoot.

More profoundly, He became a devotee of Devi Sita at first sight.

In Shri Hanuman's heart and mind, Sita was revered as a mother from the moment he beheld her. She stood beyond reproach, a figure of divine perfection. His respect, admiration, and devotion only intensified upon witnessing her dignified restraint in the face of Ravana's odious advances.

Ravana approached Sita with crafted poetry and flattering words, his mind corrupted by unrelenting desire. From the day he had abducted her, she had occupied his every waking thought. Daily, he concocted schemes, indulging in visions and fantasies about how he might persuade her to accept him.

Despite his command over countless beauties and vast riches, Ravana's inner poverty was stark. He was fixated on possessing yet another woman—a warrior princess devoted to her husband, who refused even to glance at his demonic countenance.

On seeing the emaciated, tear-streaked Sita, Ravana realised that even in her distress, she appeared more radiant than any of his queens.

If only he hadn't been cursed, he could have had his way with her, rued the lusty demon.

Ravana, unfortunately, is often celebrated as a hero by some ill-educated and psychotic humans because of their hatred for *dharma* and Rama.

It baffles me—as to what kind of consciousness would celebrate a rapist like Ravana?

Ravana tried to molest the celibate Vedvati who killed herself and procured a curse upon him. Some versions of the Ramayana also state that it was Vedvati who incarnated as Ma Sita to be the cause of the demon's end.

Upon conquering the heavens, Ravana violated the celestial Punjikasthala.

He then ended up raping Rambha, another celestial nymph who was indirectly related to him. Rambha was the partner of Nalkuvera, son of Ravana's stepbrother, Kubera. Despite her pleas to spare her and invoking the sanctity of the equation, the 'hero of all the *adharmikas*' ends up raping her. It was then that Rambha's husband procured a curse upon the demon that if he ever again attempted to violate a woman against her will, he would end up dead.

Ravana was not a gentleman lover to have not forced himself upon Sita.

Even if, for argument's sake, we assume he didn't force himself upon her out of choice, what kind of love would it be to abduct someone away, mentally harass her, and threaten death if she didn't accede?

Some others claim that Ravana abducted Sita to avenge the 'disrespect' shown by Shri Rama (and Lakshmana) to Surpanakha,

Ravana's sister, ignoring the fact that Surpanakha tried to kill Devi Sita in the first place.

It is also essential to note that *Ravana, in a fit of rage, had once killed Surpanakha's husband.*

Furthermore, Ravana, enticed by Surpanakha's description of Ma Sita's beauty, lacked the courage to face the valiant Bhagavan Shri Rama and Shri Lakshmana in direct combat. The demon king had been told by his minions that Raghuveer had single-handedly killed 14,000 rakshasha warriors.

No wonder his cowardice was evident in his choice to stealthily abduct Lord Rama's consort, underlining that true bravery would have led him to confront his adversaries openly.

Moreover, love does not equal sexual attraction.

Sex is a beautiful activity; even Bhagavan Shri Krishna explains that *kama*, or that desire that isn't in dissonance with *dharma*, is divine.

But, sensuality, when not channelised, leads only to perversion.

Devi Sita, the epitome of virtue and devotion, had absolute disgust and contempt for the demon Ravana. The powerful and cunning demon king Ravana had been relentlessly pursuing Sita.

No matter how many times he came with a proposition of glory, riches, power, and enjoyment that would have swayed the heart of any other being, Devi Sita only rebuked him. The demon, relentless in his pursuit, promised Sita the queenship of Lanka. He vowed to subjugate the entire world and gift it to Maharaj Janaka, Sita's father, in a desperate bid to win her over.

What can Rama do, asked Ravana, his voice dripping with arrogance. Most probably, Rama must have fallen dead, proclaimed the demon, underestimating Rama's strength and determination. 'Even if he manages to somehow reach the shores of Lanka, my army will finish him,' boasted Ravana, his confidence in his own power blinding him to the possibility of Rama's victory.

'Accept me as your partner,' the king of Lanka begged Sita.

Despite all his attempts to break Sita's spirit and resilience, the beloved of Shri Rama didn't budge. She felt fresh contempt and disgust form in her heart at the demon's sinful suggestion.

How can a person who's committed to her partner even think of cohabiting with someone else?

She plucked out a blade of grass, as a symbol of protection, and placed it in between her and the lusty king. This simple act was a powerful statement of her commitment and refusal to succumb to the demon's temptations.

She admonished the sinful demon. She said it seemed like there was no one in Lanka who could give sage advice. It appeared no one in Lanka had any morality or maybe the demon was immune to good counsel. As a compassionate mother, Devi Sita advised the demon to respectfully take her back to Rama and seek forgiveness. It was possible, the kind-hearted Lord Rama may spare the demon's life and kingship.

Sita spoke with scorn that pierced deeper than arrows: 'You snatched me away like a cowardly cur slinking from the sight of lions, dodging confrontation with the noble heroes. Had you dared such transgression before the eyes of those valiant brothers, they would have laid you low without a second thought.'

Devi Janaki's voice, unyielding and fierce, rang with a prophecy of doom: 'Should you seek refuge in the darkest depths of the netherworlds, know that Shri Rama's justice will find you. By forging this enmity with the mighty and virtuous Rama, you have etched your fate in stone.'

With a defiant grace, Bhagavati Sita proclaimed her power—mighty enough to reduce the wretched demon to cinders. Yet, she deemed him unworthy of the spiritual force such an act would expend.

Instead, she envisioned a fitting end crafted by her valorous husband's hand. *For Sita was to Rama as the radiant beams that dance forth from the sun—utterly inseparable and endlessly enduring.*

The veneer of the 'love-struck' Ravana, who had so far not dared to touch Sita without her consent, crumbled, revealing a violent and psychotic core. The demon king, driven to madness, contemplated striking down the captive lady, only to be stayed by the intervention of his queen, Dhanyamalini.

Dhanyamalini, playing upon his vanity, subtly chided him: 'Why covet an ordinary mortal woman when celestial beauties are at your beck and call?'

Ravana, inflamed and not to be appeased, barked orders at the demonesses guarding the Ashoka Grove. 'Intensify her torments,' he commanded, 'Use whatever means necessary to bend her will to mine.'

To Sita, he issued a chilling ultimatum. 'Submit to me within a month, or be prepared to meet a gruesome fate: my attendants will carve you up and feast on you at dawn,' threatened the deluded demon, his facade of affection now fully shattered.

How foolish was this demon? wondered Shri Hanuman.

How can one win over the goddess of fortune, Mahalakshmi (Sita is said to be an incarnation of Mahalakshmi) with the promise of wealth?

As soon as Ravana departed, the *rakshasis* began their verbal assault on Sita.

Some *rakshasis* tried to seduce her with offers of riches and power, while others told her how 'fortunate' she was to have caught the attention of their king, who had even the gods under his sway. One of them extolled Ravana's strength and charm, praising his regal bearing and handsome features.

But Devi Sita remained unmoved by their words.

When they saw that she paid them no heed, some of them resorted to threats, brandishing their weapons and threatening her with physical harm. In the face of these threats, the warrior queen stood defiant. She proclaimed that she would choose death over succumbing to the demon. She declared that her life and loyalty were dedicated only to Rama, and that she would wait for him to rescue her, steadfast in her devotion.

Shri Ramadoot was now filled with rage. He felt the anger that had been simmering within his heart since Ravana's arrival now boiling over as he witnessed the ghastly demonesses torturing Sita. The urge to leap from his hidden perch and crush the life out of them surged through Lord Hanuman. Yet, he summoned his divine wisdom to master his fury.

He understood that any sudden outburst might not only terrify Devi Sita but could also provoke the demons to whisk her away to an even more secluded location. So, he restrained himself, choosing patience over immediate action, waiting for the right moment to deliver his crucial message to Devi Sita.

In her anguish, Sita cried out, despairing under the torrent of verbal abuse from the *rakshasis*. Overwhelmed, she clung to a nearby tree, her thoughts turning piteously towards her valiant husband. 'Surely, Rama, steadfast in *dharma*, would not forsake his wife,' she reassured herself.

Sita pondered on the fate of Jatayu, the noble vulture who had perished in his valiant attempt to thwart her abduction. He must have informed her beloved Rama and his brother about her plight. Yet, why had they not yet come to her rescue?

She consoled herself with the thought that if Rama were aware of her exact location in Lanka, he would have already stormed the island, intent on reducing the golden city to ashes in his quest to rescue her. But despair gnawed at her heart as she considered another possibility—what if Rama did not know where she was?

What if, stricken by grief, he too had succumbed?

Clutching to a sliver of hope, the thought of reuniting with Rama was all that sustained Sita's spirit. She held onto the belief that someday, somehow, she would see her husband again.

In the midst of her turmoil, one *rakshashi* named Trijata stood apart, a beacon of wisdom. Untouched by the *tamasik* darkness that shrouded Lanka, much like her father Vibhishana, Trijata intervened as the demonesses unleashed their cruelty upon Sita.

Fresh from her slumber, she swiftly commanded the attention of her kin, halting their torment with the promise of an ominous dream she had witnessed.

Curiosity halted the cruelty. High above, hidden in the foliage, Anjaneya, in his mystical, diminutive form, listened intently, equally eager to decipher the contents of Trijata's vision.

Trijata, her voice heavy with the weight of premonition, began to share her vision, which seemed less a dream than a glimpse into the future. She described seeing a radiant figure, unmistakably like Lord Rama, reunited joyously with Sita. They were dressed in resplendent white, adorned with celestial garlands, aboard a magnificent aircraft resembling the *Pushpaka Vimana*— the aerial chariot of Kubera, usurped by Ravana. Together with Lakshmana, they ascended towards the north. Yet, this was not the foreboding part of her vision.

Trijata's voice grew sombre as she relayed the next segment of her dream. She saw Ravana and his ministers adorned in red, their heads shaven, descending southwards in a chariot drawn by asses—a stark contrast to the ascent of Rama and his kin. The *rakshasa* warriors seemed to vanish into a dark abyss, all except for Vibhishana, who radiated kingly virtue and splendour.

But the ominous tidings did not end there. Trijata spoke of a *mighty Vanara, leaping with a mischievous smile across the golden city, which lay in flames beneath him.*

An expert in omens, Trijata noted the signs shown by Sita herself—her left arm's palpitations and the twitching of her left eyelid, harbingers of imminent positive change. These, she declared, were clear indications of Rama's proximity and his impending rescue.

The demonesses, unversed in the interpretation of omens and dreams, found themselves disquieted by Trijata's revelations. Their interest in torment shifted to a sense of foreboding; some drifted away, others turned to intoxicants to drown their unease, and a few hastened to report to Ravana.

Devi Sita, though momentarily buoyed by Trijata's prophecy, could not entirely cast off her cloak of sorrow. Goswami Tulsidas reflects on Trijata's continued efforts to console Sita, her intuition firm that the vision would soon materialise.

As the *rakshasis* dispersed, leaving Devi Sita in her solitude, she remained engulfed in her sombre thoughts.

Observing all from his perch was Lord Hanuman, who saw this moment of quiet as his opportunity to reveal himself to Devi Sita. But just as he prepared to make his presence known, he noticed her actions with growing alarm.

It seemed Sita, in her despair, was tying her braid to a branch—could she be contemplating the unthinkable? The thought struck Anjaneya with a sharp pang of urgency.

Key Takeaway
Sometimes, Your Subconscious Holds the Key

This particular section highlights Sita's sublime character and incredible strength. One cannot imagine the mental fortitude she possessed to remain alive and resist both the temptations and threats of Ravana and company.

She was completely cut off from the rest of the world. She was repeatedly told that either she has to succumb to the lusty wretch's overtures or be eaten up. That she survived for months is a miracle.

But the most important part is how even the most powerful personality like Devi Sita was on the verge of giving up and committing suicide!

While this section of the great Ramayana once again helps us realise that life situations can sometimes turn so adverse and can render even the best among us depressed, it also serves as a powerful reminder to be kinder to ourselves and our mistakes as well.

Trijata's entry and her premonition leads us to realise that good and wise people can exist everywhere. Even in a place like Lanka, seeped with intoxicating materialism, people like Trijata and Shri Vibhihshan serve as shining examples of sanity and conscious behaviour.

Vedic civilisation has always believed in science of omens. This was also the case with other parts of the world. In a fit to prove ourselves more scientific, we started rejecting omens and intuition as dogmatic. However, it has been the experiential realisation of generations of human beings that certain omens can predict future events.

According to the theoretical science of omens, if the left side body parts are twitching or palpitating, it augurs auspiciousness for women. If this happens for males, it can indicate some danger or threat.

For men, if the right side of the body is twitching or palpitating, that augurs auspiciousness. For women, right-side twitching or palpitating can mean some negativity.

As if by divine arrangement, as I was writing the book, I experienced first hand, the merit of this omen!

I had lost an important document at work which caused a lot of emotional and financial stress. A few days before, I had ended up reading and chanting the verse for finding lost things, (see chapter 4, section 3 of the book). My right eyelid was twitching continuously. By the immaculate grace of Shri Ramayana and Shri Hanuman, it was the same day I completed writing the chapter where Hanuman locates Devi Sita. I also found the papers on that day! I was compelled to believe in the power of omens through practical realisation.

On a different note, since childhood, I have been hearing my elders speak about omens. I remember the day before my grandfather died in a road accident, my mother was concerned that her right eyelid had been twitching. She even saw a dream that induced fear and negativity. Similarly, an aunt had also been experiencing similar omens before the tragedy.

Dreams/nightmares have always piqued the curiosity of human beings. In my clinical hypnotherapy training, I was taught about different types of dreams:

1. **Sorting dreams:** A person ends up dreaming something related to the events of the day or something they'd spoken about or come across.
2. **Venting dreams:** Here a person ends up seeing random events or objects appear. These dreams, which are laced with symbols and events, seem incredulous and illogical.
3. **Predictive dreams:** Here a person can get a glance or peak into future events or even current events happening to someone else.
4. **Signal dreams:** These kinds of dreams end up leading to a discovery, providing a solution to a problem, and so on.

We have numerous historical examples and evidences of humans getting guidance via dreams. For instance:
- Mendeleev envisioned arrangement of the periodic table.
- Neils Bohr claimed the atomic model appeared to him in a dream.
- The sewing machine's design was revealed to Elias Howe.
- Paul McCartney, famous musician and member of the 'Beatles' derived the melody of *Yesterday* from a dream!
- August Kekulé got the idea of the structure of Benzene in a dream.
- Nike, the famous brand's name came to one of the associates of Phil Knight in a dream.

Personally, I too, have experienced the mystical aspect of dreams. Years back, I had a dream in which a dear friend's elder sister was going through some form of grief. Coincidentally, we got on a call the next day and I ended up asking how she was doing. My friend said she was experiencing personal struggles!

In another instance, I had a *foreboding dream* about a vehicular purchase I made almost a year and a half later. I realised about the foreboding dream later when I was going through a dream journal that I have been maintaining since many years now.

To the sceptical mind, the ideas of receiving guidance via dreams or omens can seem lunatic. However, a rational mind and may I daresay, a scientific mind, does not reject any theory without testing its merit. But how does one test these theories?

By being constantly observant and conscious. Keeping a journal, whether for dreams or otherwise is a fantastic practice that can itself serve as a powerful tool for you to find patterns in your life.

My intent in sharing about omens and dreams is not to impress upon you the ideas of mystique but to point out how these things have influenced the human psyche for ages. Even for the sceptical mind, the ideas shared can be interesting food for thought.

Your Reflection

Have you or any known person ever had any mystical experience pertaining to dreams or any kind of omens?

तरु पल्लव महुँ रहा लुकाई। करइ बिचार करौं का भाई॥

Hiding behind the leaves on a branch of the tree, Hanuman wondered how to help Sita.

Chapter 3

Rama *Katha*—Antidote to Pain

When things are going south, nothing seems to work out, and there just does not seem to be even a ray of hope; it is inevitable then that a person starts questioning his or her own choices in the past. One tends to rue one's misfortunes, wondering what had one done in the past to merit the current predicament. Some people also end up becoming bitter with everyone else. Some become bitter with themselves.

Devi Sita found herself in such a harrowing, hopeless place, revisiting the day she was abducted by the demon king. She dwelled on the moments that led to her current agony:

- Her enchantment with the golden deer.
- Her disregard for the cautious and wise counsel of her brother-in-law, Lakshmana, who suspected the deer was a shape-shifting demon.
- Her doubts about the character and intentions of her son-like brother-in-law, when he firmly believed that the mighty Lord Rama could not be overpowered by a mere demon.

It is crucial to highlight that there is no mention of a 'Lakshmana Rekha' or protective line that Devi Sita crossed, leading to her abduction in the original text of *Valmiki Ramayana*. This element was introduced in later retellings of the Ramayana.

Previously, we discussed how Shri Ramadoot, through positive self-talk, could escape the clutches of depression and suicidal thoughts. In stark contrast, we see Devi Sita spiralling further into despair, inching towards embracing such fatal thoughts due to negative self-reflection.

These moments underscore the profound power of thoughts, as beautifully articulated by Bhagavan Shri Krishna in the Bhagavad Gita, 6.5:

उद्धरेदात्मनात्मानं नात्मानमवसादयेत् ।
आत्मैव ह्यात्मनो बन्धुरात्मैव रिपुरात्मनः ॥

One must uplift themselves with the help of their mind and not degrade themselves. The mind can be both a friend and an enemy to the soul.

Trapped in a state devoid of hope, Devi Sita, who had displayed immense fortitude in enduring constant harassment and torture, now seemed on the brink of giving up.

Shri Hanuman was alarmed to see Devi Sita fastening one end of her long braid to a branch and the other around her neck, intending to end her suffering.

Vayuputra, pondering over how best to reveal himself without startling Devi Sita or drawing the attention of the nearby *rakshasis*, knew he had to act swiftly, yet cautiously. A sudden appearance in his Vanara form could shock her or worse, alert the demonesses.

Thus, *Shri Ramadoot chose a subtler approach, beginning to narrate the uplifting Shri Rama Katha and chanting the holy names* of Shri Rama—methods recommended by saints and devotees to infuse one's life with joy, wisdom, and love.

It's noted by Valmiki Muni that Lord Hanuman chose not to use Sanskrit for his narration but a local dialect, likely the one spoken in Ayodhya, to stir sweet memories within Sita's heart.

On hearing Shri Hanuman's melodious, devotional, and soul-stirring voice, all Devi Sita's worries and anxieties dissolved. She was rooted to the spot, overwhelmed by a sudden surge of hope.

Shri Ramadoot narrated Rama's life—from his birth and marriage to his exile and her abduction. He detailed Rama's alliance with Sugreeva, the slaying of Vali, and the dispatch of the Vanara and bear armies to search for her. He spoke of his own journey from the shores of Bharatvarsha to Lanka and his covert entry into the Ashoka Grove.

As he concluded his devotional narrative, Sita mentally bowed down to the source of the voice, a voice that rekindled hope and joy within her for the first time since her abduction.

Looking up, Sita scanned the tree branches and spotted a small Vanara sitting with folded palms in supplication. As she locked eyes with him, Hanuman leapt to the ground and bowed deeply, holding the Anjali Mudra above his head—a gesture of utmost respect in Vedic customs.

Shri Ramadoot then inquired, 'Are you Devi Sita, the divine consort of Shri Rama?'

Sita confirmed her identity, touching upon her lineage and her bond with Rama. Despite his diminutive form, she sensed a profound grace and power emanating from this tiny Vanara.

As Mahavir Hanuman introduced himself as the messenger of Lord Rama, a motherly affection surged within Her.

Yet, the emotional scars were deep. 'How can I know you are not Ravana? How can I trust this is not another deceit?' she asked, Her voice trembling with a mix of hope and suspicion.

Taken aback, Shri Hanuman pondered his next move. He had been cautious, mindful not to alarm her, narrating the entire Rama *Katha* and adopting a gentle form.

What more could Shri Ramadoot do to earn Sita's trust?

To win her trust, the Rudra-Avatar would need to pass another test.

Key Takeaway
Imbibe Lessons from the Scriptures

It is estimated a person has over fifty thousand thoughts per day.

How many of those thoughts are we able to keep consciously? How often do we become mindful and aware of our self-talk?

A Japanese researcher named Dr Masuro Emoto did a study with water. He proclaimed that water responds to words, prayers, and thoughts. It is described that in his study, he experimented with speaking positive words and prayers to one batch of water and used negative words with another batch. When he froze the batches of water, he found that the batch of water that got positive words and intentions produced beautiful crystal structures. The batch receiving negative words produced distorted crystals.

In the Vedic religion, much emphasis is placed on sanctified food and water, termed *prasad*. The word literally means grace. Food and water is offered to the divine with the intention of blessing the food with love. Vedic civilisation propounds the idea and understanding that we become what we consume. Food and water are essential for survival, and to spiritualise our lives easily and effectively.

It is a known historical account that the founder Acharya of Iskcon, His Divine Grace, Bhaktivedanta Swami Srila Prabhupada, transformed the hippies in New York into spiritualists (Vaishnavas), simply by feeding them Krishna-Prasad! His Divine Grace used to feed the young men and women *gulab-jamuns* that he personally prepared and offered with love to Shri Krishna. The *gulab-jamuns* later came to be known as Iskcon-bullets!

I would like to add just like food and water, there are so many other things we consume as well that define the state of our being. Our thoughts are as important, if not more important, than food and water for the quality of life we experience, the people we speak with, the media we engage with, and so on. Keeping tabs on all these things can ensure that we experience more harmony in our lives.

However, there are times we cannot navigate our thoughts, our troubles, and pains by our own selves. In such cases, we need help and we should seek it.

When our ancients thought of decoding the Vedas which were inscrutable for the masses, they started narrating the wisdom of the Vedas via stories. Foremost among them are Ramayana and Mahabharat which are called *itihās*—meaning it so happened.

These tales written by luminaries of their time, used the backdrop of historical figures of ancient Bharat to share wisdom that could reach the masses.

Regardless of age, gender, nationality, and belief systems, everyone loves a good story. If such a story can also add value, instil hope, uplift, and inspire, then that story becomes legendary. Even more so if it is based on historical accounts as is the case with Ramayana and Mahabharata.

I have personally experienced it—the tales of Ramayana and Mahabharata fill me with joy, wonder, reverence, hope, and most importantly, help me gain wisdom to deal with life's inevitable vicissitudes. That is also what inspires me to write and present this book to you.

In no way will I ever suggest or say that all we should do is narrate stories of Ramayana and Mahabharata to people experiencing challenges. I strongly recommend seeking professional and clinical help when life seems overwhelmingly morose. I too have done the same.

However, I also realise that it is not always easy, accessible, or affordable to seek therapy. It is also not common for everyone to have access to wise people. In such cases, the company of wisdom texts like Ramayana, Mahabharata and the Bhagavad Gita is invaluable, or say any other text that helps one heal and uplift.

If we do take out the time to hear, read, and immerse ourselves in ancient wisdom, we can definitely be more resilient to life's reversals.

How?

Because these scriptural texts help us realise that we are not alone. We are not the only ones who are experiencing pain or reversals in life. Even the people we bow down to and pray to have had to endure sufferings when they were around. And most importantly, by developing endurance, faith, and patience, we definitely can overcome our sufferings and see the light.

In fact, even in Mahabharata when Yuddhisthira is overcome with grief, Rishi Markandeya narrates the Ramayana to assuage him that you are not alone in grief, dear child! People of even higher calibre have gone through pain; no one is spared!

You do not have to do it all alone. Talk, seek help and guidance, and once again, it is completely natural, human or as we can notice in the story, even *divine* to breakdown.

And as Shri Hanuman demonstrates, stories can inspire.

Stories can transform and may even lead someone out of a despondent state of mind.

Your Reflection
Here are a couple of journal prompts for your reflection:
1. Think of a time, a story, any story, which made a significant impact on you. It could be a story you read, heard, or saw in the media. Write why and how that story impacted you.
2. Can you think of a time when you received wise counsel from someone when you were feeling low? Write a letter of gratitude to that person even if you cannot share it with them directly.

राम दूत मैं मातु जानकी । सत्य सपथ करुनानिधान की ॥

O Mother, I am the messenger of Shri Rama—I sincerely swear on the name of the abundantly compassionate one (Rama)

Chapter 4

The Most Blissful Test

In the shadowed depths of despair, Devi Sita, long tricked and tormented, was justifiably wary.

During her earlier time in the forest, she had encountered numerous demons capable of morphing their shapes and forms. One such demon had ultimately been the cause of her abduction.

Despite being thoroughly captivated and uplifted by Hanuman's narration of Shri Rama *Katha*, her caution prevailed, prompting her to request a description of Rama's form and appearance.

Devi Sita knew well that the cowardly Ravana lacked the courage to even gaze upon Rama in the forest. She reasoned that neither Ravana nor his minions could ever accurately depict the divine and glorious features of Shri Raghupati.

However, the saints, devotees, and scholars of the Ramayana interpret Devi Sita's request differently. They believe that on hearing Ramadoot's divine voice, Devi Sita instantly recognised its celestial origin.

The deceitful and lustful Ravana could never emulate the profound devotion with which this Vanara recounted the sacred story of Sita and Rama. Trust had been kindled, but Sita, yearning for more, did not want Shri Hanuman to cease glorifying her beloved husband.

For the first time since her separation from Rama, the tiny Vanara's words made her feel as though she was reunited with her beloved.

Eagerly, she wished to hear how this eloquent Vanara would describe the universally admired beauty of her divine husband.

Shri Ramadoot smiled, recognising the request as perhaps the simplest test he had ever faced. To speak of his revered deity was as natural to Maruti as breathing.

On being asked to depict the form of the one whose beauty even gods and Cupid admire, Lord Hanuman closed his eyes, a smile gracing his face, and began:

- Shri Rama radiates like the Sun, charming as the full moon, regal as a deity.
- He is valiant like Shri Vishnu and truthful like Brihaspati, the preceptor of the gods.
- His beauty, aura, and radiance might make one wonder if he is Cupid incarnate!
- He stands as the greatest warrior known.
- The entire universe could be shielded by this formidable hero.
- Shri Rama's brilliant face, which dims the glory of the full moon, is adorned with eyes as beautiful as freshly blossomed lotus flowers.
- He makes no distinction among beings, showing equal kindness to all.
- Skilled in political science, supremely intelligent, a knower of the Vedas, he is humble, generous, and kind, yet a fearsome adversary to his enemies.

- His voice is deep and resonant, his tall frame and physique complemented by glowing, soft skin, each limb of his body sculpted in perfect symmetry.

Listening to this divine portrayal, Devi Sita was transported into a trance, tears of gratitude and joy streaming down her face, utterly convinced of Hanuman's authenticity.

Overwhelmed with emotion, she inquired about the extraordinary bond between humans and vanaras.

Hanuman, with reverence, responded, 'It is all by your grace, O divine mother!'

Noticing Sita's puzzled expression, he elaborated, 'Do you recall, during your abduction, how you cast your jewels towards a mountain? The mountain dwellers you glimpsed were Sugreeva and his ministers, including myself. It was your grace that upon glancing at Sugreeva, his misfortunes began to wane. Following your blessing, he met Shri Rama, regained his kingdom and wife.'

Maruti then recounted the tale of Sugreeva and Rama's alliance, the demise of Vali, and the mobilisation of the search parties, culminating in his own daring journey across the ocean to Lanka.

'Rest assured, O Mother, had Shri Rama known of your whereabouts, not a moment would have been lost before he stormed the shores of Lanka to dismantle the stronghold of the vile demon,' Hanuman affirmed confidently.

With that assurance, Shri Ramadoot presented a supremely special token—a ring given by Rama, carried by Hanuman with the utmost reverence. If nothing else could convince Devi Sita of Hanuman's genuineness, this ring, engraved with the name of her Lord, certainly would.

As Sita held the ring, a wave of ecstatic bliss washed over her, a sensation of being reunited with her Rama. After enduring endless months of despair, fear, and doubt, this divinely empowered Vanara had infused her spirit with hope, joy, gratitude, and nostalgic memories.

Key Takeaway
Humility is Key to all Interactions
A very important point to note in this chapter is how Shri Hanuman offers the ring to Devi Sita.

He offered the ring to her with open palms and with the most gentle and humble demeanour. He did so because whenever someone gives out something, it more often than not puts them in a more elevated position.

Shri Ramadoot wanted Sita to pick the ring from his palms so as to signify that it is the divine mother who is choosing to accept the ring from her husband Rama and Anjaneya is a mere carrier and not someone who is giving it, *per se*.

Hanuman's humility and service attitude for each and everyone around makes him not just one of our most iconic deities, but exemplifies his sense of self-assurance and contentment as a personality.

Only a person who is self-assured and secure in his being can be free from the inherent need for appreciation and affirmation for every activity that he does.

With this act of offering the ring to Devi Sita, Shri Ramadoot earned another beautiful and powerful name in the hearts and minds of devotees:

सीता शोक विनाशकाय

(ॐ सीताशोकविनाशकाय नमः)

Shri Hanuman's magical appearance ensures that all Sita Devi's sorrows are taken away.

Your Reflection

Think of a time when an item or a piece of memorabilia induced a feeling of deep love and affection towards another loved one. Write about that experience. Why did that acquire such a special place in your life?

कपि के बचन सप्रेम सुनि उपजा मन बिस्वास। जाना मन क्रम बचन यह कृपासिंधु कर दास।।

Hearing the sweet words of the tiny vanara, Sita could firmly establish the faith that this being was devoted to Rama through mind, words and action.

Chapter 5
The Game of Life

The Shri Vaishnava (an authentic school of Bhakti yoga) acharyas share a tale that happened in another realm—the realm of the divine absolute truth, Shri Vishnu, Vaikunth or Saket.

Once, while Bhagavan Shri Vishnu lay in Yoga-Nidra, a state blending restoration, meditation, and higher consciousness, Shri Mahalakshmi Devi observed a small turtle attempting to lick the lotus feet of Shriman Narayan. Eager not to disturb her husband's rest, Shri Mahalakshmi gently shooed the turtle away.

However, when the divine couple later manifested on earth as Sita and Ramachandra, the celestial turtle also took a human form.

While Mahalakshmi and Shri Vishnu played the roles of a prince and princess in exile, the turtle became a boatman whom the divine couple encountered upon their exile from Ayodhya. When Rama requested the boatman to ferry him, Sita and Lakshmana across the river Ganga, the boatman unexpectedly refused.

His reason was both wise and witty: he had heard of Lord Rama's miracle with Ahalya, whom Rama had transformed from a stone (though scholars note she was in a vegetative, unconscious state, needing divine intervention to awaken). The boatman humorously expressed his fear that Lord Rama might turn his boat into a woman!

Rama, understanding the boatman's true intent, indulged him in this playful devotional act. He reassured the boatman that no magical transformations would occur. The boatman proposed that he would only ferry them if Rama allowed his feet to be washed, and the water, now sanctified as *charanamrita*, was shared with his family.

Delighted by the boatman's devotion, Lord Rama consented, fulfilling the boatman's long-carried wish from another realm—a wish to taste the nectar from the feet of Shri Bhagavan. For devotees, the lotus feet of the Lord are not just the grace that transcends the cycle of birth and death; they symbolise the Absolute Truth itself.

After joyously ferrying the trio across the river, Rama, devoid of all riches due to his exile, sought to reciprocate the boatman's kindness. Devi Sita, intuitively understanding her husband's desire, offered a ring precious to her, bearing the divine name of Rama.

Yet, the boatman, tears of love and gratitude in his eyes, declined any material compensation, proclaiming, 'You, too, are a boatman, my lord. When I reach your shores, you too ferry me across the cycle of birth and death—that's all I ask.'

Shri Mahavishnu, in his human guise, was touched by the devotion and affirmed the boatman's heartfelt plea.

Sita had always pondered why Lord Rama kept the ring with him, knowing he was too humble to wear something bearing his own name. She chose not to question the profound ways of her beloved. Now, as Shri Ramadoot handed her the same ring, she realised why Rama had retained it.

This ring also evoked another tender memory from Ayodhya.

Once in Ayodhya, Lord Rama had mistakenly brushed off the *sindoor* (vermillion), a symbol signifying marriage, from Sita's forehead. Considering it inauspicious, Sita became angry at her husband, but Rama didn't make any efforts to pacify his wife. Their cold war continued for a while until one day, Devi Sita intentionally dropped the same ring on the floor.

Knowing Rama was within earshot, Sita called out, 'Can anyone help me find my ring?' The chivalrous Raghuveer immediately jumped into action and found the ring. As he handed it back, the divine couple exchanged a sweet smile, thus ending their loving cold war.

Just as the ring was a catalyst to unite them in Ayodhya, it reunited them once again in Lanka.

But Sita's heart was heavy with questions. Overwhelmed with emotions, she wondered why Rama had not yet come to rescue her.

Does Rama still love and care for her?

What holds him back from coming to her?

Key Takeaway
Rama, the Perfect Divine Avatar
The popularity of both the Ramayana, and of course, Lord Rama is testimony to how profoundly he connects to each section of society, irrespective of caste, creed, or occupation. He even connects with birds and animals!

- *He offers reprieve of the ascetic Ahalya. He becomes friends with the chief of the tribal community, Guha. His association with Jatayu is also special.*
- *He gives even a vulture a funeral like he would for a father.*
- *He ate in the house of the great yogini Shabari, who belonged to a forest tribe.*
- *He established friendships with Vanaras and bears.*
- *He offers shelter to even his enemy's brother.*
- *He ensures a royal funeral even for the man who caused immense pain to him and his wife.*

The point often missed and overlooked both by critics and even devotees is that Lord Rama is celebrated because of his actions and not just because he was an avatar or a divine manifestation.

Lord Rama's character, behaviour, and interactions with each and every person that he comes across exemplifies his grace, kindness, compassion, and the gift of making everyone feel at ease. This is what makes Rama an icon for all ages.

When Maharaja Dashrath, father of Rama decided to crown his son as the next king, he called a meeting with his council of ministers and the most prominent citizens from all sections of society. He asked them what was their opinion of his son, Rama, and why they felt that Rama deserved to be the next king.

The ministers and citizenry were united in their praise and glorification of Rama. Their enthusiasm about the prospect of crowning Rama as the king is such that even Maharaja Dashrath is taken aback!

Were these people tired of seeing him on the throne?

But the reason for Rama's popularity and love was revealed by the citizens only.

'Rama celebrates with us when we are happy and He is there to shed a tear when we are sad. He shares both our grief and joy.'

It is this humane characteristic in Ram that is the key for him being endearing to anyone and everyone.

Our scriptures do not celebrate a personality just because he happens to be an avatar. It is an avatar's activities, character, pastimes, and dealings with people that make the avatar lovable and venerable as well.

Bhagavan Rama's aura, his dealings, compassion, and very simply the love that he carried in his heart was what attracted everyone to his being.

Stories like that of the boatman signify how God is above and beyond petty human identities of caste, position, class and so on. God is for everyone and of everyone. The path of love, path of devotion, is open for everyone.

As Goswami Tulsidas masterfully writes:
'हरि को भजे सो हरि को होई
जात पात पूछे नहीं कोई'

Your Reflection

Think about how you connect to God or the universe. Has there ever been a time when you have felt divine grace in your life journey? Describe this experience.

Chapter 6

I Can Take You to Rama

Shri Hanuman explained to Devi Sita that the only reason Rama had not destroyed the evil, lusty king and rescued her was because there was no confirmation of her location or word about her survival. Without confirmation, it wouldn't have been wise to get the Vanaras and bears to attack a foreign location. Now that Hanuman had ascertained her location, he would return to his master, and Rama would not waste a single moment to come to her aid.

To further establish trust, and faith in Devi Sita's heart on how much Rama loved her, Lord Hanuman described Lord Rama's state:

'Lord Rama constantly thinks only about You. He cannot eat or sleep properly. One can notice him sitting in silence, staring into the distant horizon, often even oblivious to everyone and everything around him. Often, he calls out your name and sheds tears of pain.

जनि जननी मानहु जिय ऊना । तुम्ह तें प्रेमु राम के दूना ॥

Trust me, O Mother, Shri Rama loves you more than you can ever imagine!'

Hanuman's description of Lord Rama's state of mind filled Devi Sita both with relief and grief.

Hearing Hanuman describe Rama's love for her, Sita felt relief. But the grief came from hearing about Lord Rama's pitiable state caused by her absence.

Devi Sita tearfully asked Hanuman to bring Rama to Lanka as soon as possible. Time was running out; the demon had given her a year's time to submit to him. Only two months remained.

Sita explained how Ravana had completely shut out the voice of reason. She had heard that good people like Vibhishana had tried to counsel the demon and show him the path of righteousness, but the king of Lanka didn't pay heed to any good advice. If Rama did not come soon, Sita revealed that she would have to give up her life.

Hanuman was alarmed at Sita's words. He couldn't bear to imagine her in danger.

He declared: 'Let me take you to Shri Rama this very instant. You can climb on my back, Mother, and I will fly you to Shri Rama. I can even carry entire Lanka on my back, O mother. You do not worry.'

Shri Ramadoot's words put a genuine smile on Sita's face. How can this tiny Vanara manage to carry me all across this vast ocean, she wondered.

Hanuman had thus far revealed only his tiny form to Devi Sita. He didn't want to unnecessarily display his might and prowess without any valid reason in front of Sita. Shri Ramadoot's task was to give his master's message, and his spontaneous desire on seeing Sita was to hear the word 'son' from her. Now, the time was to show her that her *son* was not an ordinary, tiny Vanara.

Chanting the names of his beloved Lord Rama, Mahavir expanded himself to a gigantic form. The form was so huge that it appeared as if a mountain had suddenly appeared before Sita's eyes.

कनक भूधराकार सरीरा । समर भयंकर अतिबल बीरा ।।

As Goswami Tulsidas describes, 'Hanuman looked like

a golden mountain. His mere form could induce fear and palpitation in the enemy rank.'

Hanuman told Devi Sita, 'If need be, I can uproot this city and all the demons and throw them at the feet of Shri Raghuveer.'

She gaped in wonder at the power and prowess of the Rudra Avatar. She praised him and compared him to be as mighty as the wind god himself!

Sita wondered what was the actual size of this mystical being. To that query, Hanuman said, 'I am neither tiny nor gigantic. I assume my form as per the need of Shri Rama and his cause.'

He humbly mentioned to Sita that his significance and power comes only through serving Rama.

Hanuman's words touched Devi Sita's heart. She felt a great deal of motherly affection for this mystical being. This Vanara was not just intelligent, but extremely powerful and humble.

To further stir hope and assure Sita, Maruti mentioned that there were even more powerful beings than him in Rama's (Sugreeva's) army. Looking at Anjaneya's mighty form and hearing his words, Sita felt assured that the Vanara army would prove to be more than a match for the demons.

However, Devi Sita placed some arguments against going with the Vayuputra.

First, she mentioned how she feared falling off as Hanuman flies through the sky.

Second, the demons would awaken from their intoxication and chase them. It would be quite a hassle for Maruti to ward them off while also ensuring her safety.

Third, and most importantly, she explained the real reason she did not wish to go with Hanuman.

What was the reason?

Key Takeaway
Don't Let Doubts Put You Down

In all these months of separation from her husband and the mental and emotional torture she went through, Devi Sita's mind must have gone through a flurry of thoughts and doubts.

What if Rama never comes?

What if he abandons me?

What if he cannot forgive me for mistreating Lakshmana before the demon abducted me?

What if he had found someone else?

What if he himself perished in the grief of separation?

And all her thoughts were valid.

It was a norm in that era for kings and princes to have multiple wives. Lord Rama, however, was a unique personality, a path-breaker whose love for Sita was such that he had promised not to marry again. Lord Rama not only kept his promise in her absence when Ravana abducted her, but he also remained celibate and single, even after Sita's second exile from Ayodhya.

When Maricha, in the form of a golden deer, had lured Rama away from Panchvati, Sita was concerned about his safety. When Rama struck down the demon, Maricha mimicked Rama's voice to call out to Lakshmana and Sita for help.

The demon's trick worked, as Sita asked Lakshmana, to go to Lord Rama's aid. Lakshmana who was well aware of the trickery of the demons and also of the mighty prowess of his elder brother refused to leave her presence. Lord Rama had given clear instructions to Lakshmana that in no situation was he to leave Sita alone.

Sita ended up being extremely rude to Lakshmana, and in a fit of emotionally driven rage, had made unpalatable accusations that shattered the sincere and pure Lakshmana's heart.

In all the months of staying in Lanka, Sita's heart must have replayed that scene of chastising Lakshmana again and again. She wondered if the brothers would have forgiven her.

But this is where the beauty of the Ramayana and the beauty of the relationships between the characters shines through. Not once does Lakshamana ever again mention the incident to either his brother or sister-in-law. Not once does even Rama accuse Sita of being unreasonable to their son-like brother.

What Ramayana teaches us, and what we can gain from reading about the interactions of these personalities with each other is that one moment of anger, one moment of harshness cannot and should not wipe away years of good memories.

Sita was unreasonable in her chastisement of Lakshmana, but Lakshmana knew that Sita was being harsh only out of her love and concern for Rama. He did not take her outburst personally.

Devi Sita, on her part, felt remorse at her harsh treatment of Lakshmana, recalling how he had selflessly served both her and Rama with devotion. Both personalities thought of the other's goodness, and that ensured that they had a strong bond until the end.

Similarly, we should remember that our near and dear ones may get a bit loony sometimes. They may be unreasonable or erratic, but that should not cloud over all the good that they would have added to us in the past. Learning to forgive and understand the other's anger is what makes relationships last.

An important and practical caveat is that not everyone will deserve our forgiveness and second chance. Only our dearest people, the ones whom we trust and know are largely kind and loving are allowed that leeway to go loony once in a while. Giving someone the license to make mistakes should not mean the mistakes keep on repeating, and there isn't even a trace of remorse.

Another key lesson from this section is Shri Hanuman's sense of self-assurance. Only a person who is immensely self-secure will have no need to keep displaying their glory.

Hanuman could have appeared in his gigantic form and boasted about his strength to Devi Sita as soon as she recognised him to be an authentic person and a messenger of her husband.

However, throughout our journey with Shri Hanuman—right from the time we started, until now—one thing remains consistent, and that is his humility.

What we learn from Shri Ramadoot is that humility does not equate to lack of ability.

Hanuman's humility is to grow in stature according to the need of the hour, not shying away from work, not being overwhelmed by situations, and to be sincere in work.

Also, a personal lesson that has been most significant to my life journey has been that:

Humility does not mean a lack of self-worth, but knowing and realising that there are other contributing factors to our abilities.

To take a modern-day example: Humility is how Roger Federer used to perform on a tennis court.

Humility is how Sachin Tendulkar used to play on the cricket field.

These people were masters of their game and always made an effort to play to the best of their ability, but one couldn't detect even an iota of ego in their beings.

Such reflections and realisations make me wonder if only the truly gifted, talented, secure and great beings can afford to be truly humble.

Furthermore, any conscious and aware human understands that all their strength, glory, and prowess are gifts from a universal source/God. We can only be blessed instruments in expressing that power, glory, and prowess.

Your Reflection

What constitutes humility for you?

Who have you known and observed to be truly humble in your life?

सुनु माता साखामृग नहिं बल बुद्धि बिसाल । प्रभु प्रताप तें गरुड़हि खाइ परम लघु ब्याल ॥

O Mother (Sita Ma), a Vanara like me does not have great strength or intelligence on my own. But by the grace of my Lord (Shri Rama), even a tiny snake can devour Garuda, the mighty eagle.

Chapter 7
Remind Rama of the Crow

A sincere exploration of the Ramayana reveals the legendary love between Devi Sita and Lord Rama, a relationship steeped in profound sacrifice and relentless effort. Their story, while heartbreakingly poignant, offers a timeless testament to devotion that transcends mere reciprocation.

However, for those accustomed to viewing relationships through a transactional lens, seeking only to gauge what might be gained, the depth of Sita and Rama's love may elude understanding.

Sita's refusal to leave with Hanuman is not rooted in fear of the journey or doubt in Maruti's ability to protect her from demons. Her decision is instead a deliberate choice, aiming to ensure that the honour and triumph of rescuing her and defeating the demon are attributed rightfully to Rama.

Throughout history, judgemental attitudes have pervaded, critiquing leaders and heroes with undue harshness. Devi Sita knew that if she were rescued by Hanuman, it might lead people to question Lord Rama's capability as a protector, not just of his consort but of his future kingdom.

Moreover, the demon had caused immense suffering not only to Sita and, by extension, to Rama, but his tyranny had also afflicted the entire planet. As a future king and a Kshatriya, it was Lord Rama's dharma to uphold justice and restore order.

Sita felt that her acceptance of Shri Hanuman's offer would lead people to scoff that a deer had tricked Rama at Panchvati, leading to her abduction, and now a Vanara was needed to reunite them. Her concern was not so much her own suffering but the potential defamation of Rama.

Such are the mystifying ways of these divine beings!

Understanding Devi Sita's perspective, Shri Ramadoot agreed that it was fitting for Rama himself to come and vanquish Ravana.

Hanuman then pondered how to prove to Lord Rama and the others back in Kishkindha that he had indeed met Devi Sita. Just as Lord Rama had given him a ring to establish a connection with Sita, Hanuman felt it appropriate that Devi Sita provide him with something to show to his master.

Responding to Hanuman's request, Sita shared a deeply personal incident from their time in Chitrakoot, known only to the divine couple. She assured him that upon hearing this story, Lord Rama would need no further proof of their meeting.

Years ago, while in Chitrakoot, Shri Rama was resting with his head in Sita's lap when a persistent crow began pecking at her. Out of love for her husband, Devi Sita tried to fend off the bird quietly, but it wounded her, drawing blood. Awakened by her cry and the sight of her blood-soaked garments, Lord Rama's fury was unlike any seen before.

With his mastery of *Dhanur-vidya* and *Mantra-Shastra*, Bhagavan Rama turned a simple blade of grass into a weapon, imbuing it with the force of a *Brahmastra*, and launched it at the crow. The crow, identified in the Puranas as Jayant, son of

Indra, found no refuge, not even among the gods, as the weapon relentlessly pursued him.

Jayant, endowed with mystical abilities from his birth as the son of the king of heavens, found himself in dire straits. Fleeing from the relentless Brahmastra unleashed by Shri Rama, he sought refuge with his father, Indra. However, recognising the gravity of his son's error, Indra refused protection, admitting his own powerlessness against the divine weapon of Lord Rama.

Desperate, Jayant then turned to his mother, Devi Sachi. On learning of her son's misdeeds, she insisted that it was only right for Jayant to face the consequences of his actions. She emphasised that enduring punishment from Lord Rama would serve as a crucial lesson against the misuse of power and privilege.

Rebuffed by his parents, Jayant approached other deities, hoping for sanctuary. Yet, one by one, they too declined, each feeling unequipped to withstand Rama's wrath. Undeterred, Jayant sought an audience with Shri Brahma, the creator. But even in this exalted court, he was met only with a stern, disapproving gaze that offered no comfort or escape.

In his final bid for safety, Jayant approached Yogishwar, Bhagavan Shiva, the God of all gods. Shiva, with a knowing chuckle at the crow's folly and audacity, laid bare a profound truth: not even the combined might of the gods could counteract Lord Rama's power on the battlefield. Rama's arms, blessed with invincible strength, and his arsenal, were beyond challenge.

Bholenath advised Jayant that his only chance of salvation lay in seeking forgiveness from the very beings he had wronged. He counselled the crow to return and throw himself at the mercy of Devi Sita and Lord Rama if he wished to preserve his life.

When Jayant came seeking shelter, Lord Rama, persuaded by *Jagat-janani,* Mahalakshmi Sita's compassionate plea, withdrew the weapon but took one of Jayant's eyes as a lasting reminder of his actions.

With this story, Devi Sita implored Hanuman to convey her pain to Rama, questioning how he could tolerate her suffering when he had once unleashed a weapon across the universe for a lesser offence.

Moved by her pain, Ramadoot assured her that Shri Rama, separated from his Shakti, had forgotten the strength of his arms, but the reminder of her would invigorate him. Soon, Lord Rama would launch into action and hasten to liberate her.

Consoled by Shri Rama Doot's words, Devi Sita urged Hanuman to remind her husband of his divine prowess, recalling how Rama single-handedly defeated the 14,000-strong demon army of Khara and Dushana at Panchvati.

Reflecting on cherished memories of her beloved, Sita prepared to share more heartfelt incidents from Ayodhya, weaving the past with the present in anticipation of their future reunion.

Key Takeaway
It is in Giving that We Receive
- *Think of how easily Rama accepts the unfair exile to the forest with a smile as if he was being asked to leave for a holiday! Think of how Bharat rejects an abundant kingdom and kingship as if it were an abomination. Think of the sacrifice made by Devi Sumitra, Lakshmana's mother, and Urmila, his wife. They selflessly allowed Lakshmana to leave with Sita and Shri Rama so that he could serve his beloved brother and sister-in-law in their time of need.*
- *Sita is willing to stay longer in Lanka to ensure that the fame and glory of defeating Ravana goes to her husband.*

Ramayana teaches us the secret sauce of sustaining healthy, harmonious, and enriching relationships—to have a service attitude and think of the other's well-being while acting.

A very important point to be noted and considered here is that efforts made by these personalities did not go unappreciated, unacknowledged and were reciprocated back as well.

It is my firm belief backed by my experiences and cemented

further through readings of the Ramayana—that happy, healthy, and harmonious relationships create heaven on earth.

As Saint Francis of Assisi mentions in a famous prayer: 'It is in giving that we receive.'

Jayant's tale is a reminder to never assume oneself to be so big that no matter what transgression you end up doing, it will not attract punishment. In this day and age, we see many entitled brats who think they are above the law because of their family's influence. However, while transgressors may escape punishment in earthly courts, escaping karmic repercussion is impossible. In Jayant's case, it was instant! His transgression and repentance, Sita's forgiveness, and Rama's wrath serve as a reminder that nature believes in delivering justice and laws of karma are absolute.

Depending on what kind of action and karma we perform, the कर्म-फल is guaranteed, be it good or bad.

Your Reflection

Do you have a person who matters immensely in your life? Based upon the learnings and teachings of the Ramayana, write how you can enhance that relationship. Also, how can you serve your near and dear ones? May Sita, Rama, Lakshmana and Hanuman bless you with abundant, joyous and happy relationships in life.

कछुक दिवस जननी धरु धीरा । कपिन्ह सहित अइहहिं रघुबीरा ॥

O Ma, please be patient for some more time, Shri Rama will arrive soon with his army of Vanaras.

Chapter 8

May You Always Be Dear to Rama

During their time of exile in the forest, a tender moment unfolded when Rama noticed that Sita's vermillion, applied symbolically on her forehead, was inadvertently smudged. With a gentle and playful spirit, Rama picked up a piece of red ore from the ground and grinding the stone between his hands to create a paste, he lovingly applied it not just to her forehead, but adorned her cheeks as well. This intimate gesture, shared privately between the divine couple, was one of the memories Sita now entrusted to Hanuman.

In another recollection, Devi Sita reminisced about a day back in Ayodhya when Rama returned home later than usual. Feeling slightly vexed at the delay, and as a playful form of reprimand, she decided to bind Rama's hands with a garland of flowers, effectively making him her 'prisoner'.

However, upon noticing that even the soft flowers caused his delicate skin to redden, her heart softened, and the playful punishment turned into a moment of deep affection.

Sita relayed these incidents to Hanuman to ensure that there would be no doubt in Rama's mind that his devoted servant had truly met his beloved wife.

In addition to these tales, Devi Sita provided Hanuman with a tangible token of their encounter—the चूड़ामणि, a cherished hair ornament.

This ornament, given to her by her mother as a wedding gift and deeply valued by Sita, had been safeguarded even when she parted with other ornaments while flying over the Rishimukha mountain during her abduction.

Handing it over to Anjaneya, she ensured that Rama would recognise the undeniable proof of their meeting.

Shri Hanuman accepted the चूड़ामणि with immense reverence, recognising the profound trust and blessing it represented.

Sita, with the weight of her many months in captivity bearing down upon her, issued a dire ultimatum through Maruti:

If Rama did not arrive within a month, she would relinquish her mortal form.

The gravity of this statement alarmed Hanuman, who knew the challenges of rallying Rama's forces quickly enough to meet her deadline. However, he reassured Sita that no time would be wasted, and soon she would witness the downfall of Ravana and his oppressive regime.

As Maruti prepared to depart, Sita, with a mother's affection, blessed him abundantly. She bestowed upon him the gifts of:

Eternal youth—अजर,

Immortality—अमर,

And a wealth of virtues—गुण-निधि.

Yet, feeling his heart still yearning for more (love for his beloved deity), she added that he would always be dear to Rama and succeed effortlessly in all his endeavours.

Maruti, moved by these profound blessings, felt a renewed vigour. His heart soared, and tears of gratitude flowed as he bowed deeply before Devi Sita, whose presence had revitalised his spirit.

Sita wished her divine son could have stayed longer. His short stay in Lanka and their conversation had given Sita a new lease of life. But she knew that the sooner Vayuputra went back, the sooner Rama could arrive in Lanka.

However, the supremely intelligent Maruti was suddenly struck with an idea. Now that he had Mahalakshmi Swaroopa Devi Sita's blessings, Shri Hanuman felt even more confident. He decided that he still had one last thing to do here in Lanka and couldn't leave just yet.

He had assuaged Sita and conveyed Rama's message, which put his mind at peace. Technically, his seemingly impossible mission was now over. Now, the Vayuputra had a mischievous idea. He didn't want to leave Lanka without creating a stir.

Goswami Tulsidas narrates that Hanuman after receiving Sita's blessings sought her permission to eat some fruits. It had been a strenuous journey, without a break. The succulent and ripe fruits from Ravana's gardens looked appealing.

Brimming with motherly affection, Sita consented to his wish but cautioned him about the fierce *rakshasa* warriors guarding the grove.

Unfazed, Maruti assured her that with her blessings and the remembrance of Rama, no foe could deter him.

This pause in Maruti's departure raises questions about his priorities—given the urgency of Sita's situation and his capabilities as a yogi, shouldn't he have been unaffected by worldly needs like hunger or fatigue?

What profound reasons might Hanuman have for prolonging his stay in Lanka, despite the ticking clock? It's something to think about.

Key Takeaway
Devotion Colours the Soul with Faith

Lord Hanuman had arrived in a foreign land, looking for someone he had never met, who was suspicious, cautious, and depressed from her continued suffering. Our hero not only manages to find her amidst heavy vigilance, but also talks to her and convinces her that he was a messenger of her Rama, uplifting her negative frame of mind.

In the rich tapestry of devotion that colours the lives of those who follow Bhagavan Rama, there is a cherished folklore that beautifully illustrates the humility and magnificence of his closest devotees.

One playful day, Lord Rama, ever the orchestrator of divine lessons, posed a seemingly simple yet profound question to his two dearest devotees, Lakshmana and Hanuman. He inquired, 'Who among you is the greater devotee?'

This question was not merely a test of their humility, but also a divine setup to highlight their unparalleled devotion.

Without a moment's hesitation, Hanuman responded, declaring that it was undoubtedly, Lakshmana.

He passionately articulated Lakshmana's unparalleled devotion, which shone brightly through his sacrifices: forsaking the comforts of the palace, the companionship of his wife, and even the necessity of sleep, all to serve Rama and Sita with unyielding fidelity.

'None can match the depth of devotion, the purity of surrender, and the magnitude of greatness embodied by Lakshmana,' Hanuman proclaimed with profound respect.

Lakshmana, in turn, offered a compelling counterpoint that underscored the exceptional nature of Hanuman's devotion. With a reflective tone, he presented a powerful example.

'Consider this,' Lakshmana mused, 'Sita, despite years of familiarity, could not fully place her trust in me, yet Hanuman, meeting her for the first time, won her trust almost instantly!'

'Who then,' Lakshmana continued, his voice filled with admiration, 'can truly compare to the glory and intelligence of Hanuman? His ability to earn the trust of Sita so swiftly is a testament to his supreme devotion and sagacity.'

This folklore not only celebrates the inherent humility and magnanimity of both Lakshmana and Hanuman, but also shows Lakshmana's keen observation, highlighting the profound impact of Hanuman's brief interaction with Devi Sita.

Buoyed by blessings, Shri Rama Naam (प्रभु मुद्रिका मेलि मुख माहीं । जलधि लांघि गए अचरज नाहीं ॥) and by the dint of his mystical prowess, the son of Vayu crossing the vast expanse of the ocean is one thing. But Shri Hanuman's sensitivity and what we now term as Emotional Quotient (EQ) are worth marvelling at.

A conclusion that we can safely derive from this section of our story is that *success is not solely skill-dependent*.

As we noticed in the earlier section and chapter, even the mammoth effort of crossing over the ocean and dealing with distractions and obstacles wasn't enough. Even a being with the powers of Hanuman had to take recourse to prayers to finally locate Sita.

Further, talents and abilities usher in success only when a person is grounded, humble, and has a robust, emotional intelligence.

Had Shri Hanuman only depended on his physical powers, He may have scared Devi Sita, or worse, alerted demons before getting to meet Her.

Talent, success, and prowess can never bring lasting and enduring success. It is only when these attributes are combined with humility and emotional intelligence that a person can leave a legacy of lasting success.

Another vital point to consider is how unconditional and loving service brings abundant blessings in their wake. Hanuman selflessly wanted to serve not just Rama, but also his friend Sugreeva, the other Vanaras, and bears, as well. He tried to bring joy and peace to each person in his life.

Even when he met Devi Sita, all he wanted to hear from her was the word, 'son'.

Pleased by Shri Ramadoot's purity and service, Sita not only addresses him as son but pours divine blessings on him.

In another iconic folklore, we learn that in the glorious aftermath of the war with Ravana, as Sita, Rama, and Lakshmana triumphantly returned to Ayodhya, a grand coronation was held to celebrate Rama's ascension to the throne. Amidst the festivities and jubilation, Rama and Sita sought to express their deep gratitude to those who had stood by them during their trials.

As they distributed gifts to honour the contributions of each ally, they found themselves pondering over what would be a suitable gift for Shri Hanuman, their beloved son whose devotion knew no bounds. How could any earthly gift possibly reflect their immense gratitude to Maruti, whose selfless love had been a beacon of hope and strength?

Sita, moved by her affection and respect for Hanuman, decided to gift him a pearl necklace that she had worn around her neck—a gift of great sentimental and material value.

The assembly of Ayodhya watched in awe as this priceless treasure was bestowed on Hanuman. While some murmured, questioning what the Vanara had done to deserve such an honour, those who had witnessed his valour and dedication during the war understood the depth of his contributions.

However, the real surprise came when Shri Hanuman, on receiving the necklace, began to dismantle it, inspecting each pearl closely as if searching for something within.

This peculiar behaviour baffled the onlookers, some of whom mocked the gesture, cynically questioning the wisdom of gifting such a precious item to a Vanara. Could a forest-dweller truly appreciate such a refined gift?

Rama, ever perceptive of his devotee's heart, stepped forward to address the confusion. With a gentle voice, he asked Hanuman why he had chosen to break apart the necklace given by Sita.

Hanuman's response resonated with profound devotion and became legendary among bhakti yogis. 'I was looking for you and Sita, my Lord,' he declared. 'What use is any material possession if it does not serve as a reminder of you?'

To silence any lingering doubts among the sceptics in the crowd, Hanuman took a dramatic step. With his sharp nails, he tore open his chest, revealing an image that left the assembly in awe—an image of Sita and Rama lovingly imprinted upon his heart.

This poignant folktale not only underscores the depth of Shri Hanuman's devotion but also teaches us a profound lesson: that unconditional love for the divine attracts an unceasing supply of abundant blessings. In our day-to-day lives, when we are looking to help others or be of service, we can always gain inspiration by reminding ourselves of Hanuman.

We learn from Shri Ramadoot how to be selfless and employ our abilities to be of service to others. We learn to give for the sake of giving, not just for payback. We learn that when we work in life with elevated intention, the universe blesses us beyond imagination.

For the *astikas* and devotees, I say, let us aim to not just worship and be ritualistic but also imbibe the lessons and teachings of our legends and deities. And to the curious reader and agnostic, I humbly suggest that there is immense wisdom to be gained from ancient scriptures if our intention is to grow in life.

Your Reflection

Has there ever been a time in your life when you helped someone without expectation? How did it make you feel? Do you think you can detach yourself from the outcome when you help someone?

रावण त्रास दई सिय को सब, राक्षसी सों कही सोक निवारो ।
ताहि समय हनुमान महाप्रभु, जाए महा रजनीचर मारो ।
चाहत सीय असोक सों आगि सु, दै प्रभु मुद्रिका सोक निवारो
को नहीं जानत है जग में कपि, संकटमोचन नाम तिहारो ॥

Ravan was tormenting Sita by instructing his demonesses to torture her. At that moment you arrived and disposed off many evil demons. You handed out Shri Rama's ring to Ma and relieved her of her emotional suffering. Who in the world doesn't know your name, Sankat Mochan— the queller of misery!

Chapter 1

Monkeying Around

With the deadline looming, it was expected that Vayuputra would soar back to Lord Rama to relay Devi Sita's message and convey her precarious state. However, Shri Hanuman chose to linger in Lanka a bit longer, driven by a multitude of strategic and heartfelt reasons.

Hanuman was both fascinated and awed by Lanka's splendid fortifications. During his extensive search for Devi Sita, he had meticulously mapped out Lanka's strategic defence outposts. Yet, he yearned to test the robustness of the Lankan defence forces further.

Hanuman observed that the kingdom's military, while formidable, harboured a complacency by assuming their state to be impregnable. But, herein, Hanuman saw an opportunity to test the military's invincibility.

This became the primary reason for his extended stay: to challenge the might of Lankan warriors and scrutinise their defence system in action.

Second, the dire state and misery of Sita had deeply touched Shri Ramadoot, her newly found son. Fuelled by a righteous indignation, Maruti yearned to confront those who dared traumatise Sita, seeking to alleviate some of the injustice she was enduring.

Third, Shri Hanuman pondered the significant impact of defeating the demons single-handedly. Such a feat could potentially demoralise Ravana and his forces, perhaps even pushing the reasonable citizens of Lanka to pressure Ravana into reconsidering his actions and negotiating peace with Shri Rama, thereby avoiding further conflict.

Reason number four was rooted in bolstering Sita's spirits. If news of her son single-handedly wreaking havoc on Lanka's army reached her, it would surely ignite a surge of confidence in her heart about the capabilities of the Vanara army aiding her divine husband.

Reason number five ties back to Hanuman's divine origins as an incarnation of Bhagavan Shiva. Ravana, having once been *forced* to offer prayers to Mahadev and gaining powers in return, was now on a path that needed divine correction. Shiva, who is impartial and benevolent to all, desired to guide Ravana away from destruction. Shri Hanuman, embodying the will of Mahadev, saw this as a critical moment to influence Ravana directly, perhaps even knocking sense into the demon king's lust-driven pursuits.

Empowered by the blessings and darshan of Devi Sita, Vayuputra leapt towards Ravana's favourite garden, housing the most divine fruits. Yet, his intent was less about savouring these delights and more about causing a spectacle.

Assuming his mighty form, Lord Hanuman embarked on a chaotic spree, reminiscent of a mischievous child tearing through a set of Legos. The walls crumbled, archways fell, and trees were uprooted and tossed into ponds. Clearly, Maruti's appetite was for destruction, not for fruit!

The havoc roused the guards and demonesses from their slumber, with Mahavir's roars spreading fear throughout the palace. Lanka's most magnificent garden was laid waste within minutes, leaving everything destroyed except for the area and tree sheltering Sita.

Confused and terrified, the demonesses tasked with guarding Sita bombarded her with questions, hinting at Trijata's earlier warnings about provoking this powerful human lady. The questions flew fast:

Who is this being? Do you know him? How is he related to you? Was he speaking to you before his rampage?

The exploits of her son brought immense joy to Devi Sita's heart. Managing to suppress a smile, she cleverly deflected, suggesting that the fearsome figure might just be one of their own, given their mastery of disguise. She feigned ignorance, claiming that his gigantic form had frightened her too much to look directly at him.

With the guards incapacitated and the grove in ruins, the demonesses had no choice but to report this embarrassing breach to Ravana.

Key Takeaway
Be Like Hanuman

Lord Hanuman wasn't asked to test the might of Ravana's army, destroy his favourite garden, or instil fear in the hearts of the demons before Lord Rama arrived. But he does all this and more.

Each and every act of this mighty, saintly hero of ours was aimed for another's wellbeing. His calculated antics in the grove were not meant to show his prowess or might but to send a message to the demons that they weren't as unconquerable as they thought themselves to be. Hanuman is termed as ज्ञानिनामग्रगण्यम् and बुद्धिमतां वरिष्ठ by scholars, meaning, he is considered to be the greatest amongst thinkers and the most intelligent.

One person may have physical might, and another may have profound intelligence, but the glory of Lord Hanuman is the perfect combination of might, intelligence, and most importantly, the perfect understanding of when and how to use his abilities.

Hanuman is the kind of person who will not only accomplish the task assigned but have the foresight to accomplish even more. Hanuman is a dream corporate employee, one might even say!

Shri Ramadoot had noticed the might of the defence system of Lanka. Observing Ravana's dealing with Sita, he felt that the demon was too intoxicated by power and lust to realise his mistake and seek a truce. War seemed inevitable.

These demons of Lanka assumed they were unassailable and that they could never be threatened by puny humans or Vanaras. Demons considered humans and Vanaras as lower forms of life that could even be consumed as food by them. Ravana's empire had been built upon bullying the weak, establishing a *'My way or highway system,'* and assuming that none could match them.

Hanuman wanted to send a strong message that no matter how mighty or powerful or talented one may be, the universe has a way of humbling everyone. History is replete with such examples—in politics, sports, and in cinema.

Ravana's ego and eventual downfall owing to it is such a powerful example that there is a Hindi saying around it. I have noticed whenever someone becomes unbearably boastful and egotistical, people say: घमंड तो रावण का भी नहीं चला—meaning, the mighty Ravana, who had conquered even gods, was humbled; then who are we to be intoxicated with ego?

If Shri Ramadoot managed to make a dent in the demon's ego, display the might of Rama (as his representative), and test the strength of the Lankan warriors, then Rama and his army would have a head start when the war eventually began.

Our lesson is to remain humble about our achievements and abilities. Keep a constant vigilance on your inner dialogue and its subsequent manifestation in our outer behaviour with others.

Another significant episode in this chapter is Devi Sita lying about knowing Hanuman. Why did Sita lie?

Lord Rama and Devi Sita are the symbols of morality and *dharma*. Lying is not considered to be an act of dharma. To answer this question, let us try and understand the Vedic perspective on the topic. In the *Srimad Bhagavatam* (8.19.43), Shukracharya outlines instances where a lie is acceptable.

स्त्रीषु नर्मविवाहे च वृत्त्यर्थे प्राणसङ्कटे ।
गोब्राह्मणार्थे हिंसायां नानृतं स्याज्जुगुप्सितम् ॥

Playful banter amidst lovers, jokingly, for the sake of marriage, to earn one's livelihood, to protect oneself, or our cows, or to protect someone else from danger, then falsehood is not condemned.

Here, Sita utters a lie for the sake of her son. If Ravana had learned that Hanuman had come to meet Sita, he would have been enraged beyond measure. Out of motherly compassion, to protect her son, Ma Sita lied. Sita trusted her son to have a plan for whatever he was looking to achieve through his mystical antics.

A knife in the hands of a surgeon can save a life, and in the hands of a criminal, take one. Similarly, killing someone is abominable, but a soldier shooting down an enemy to defend his homeland is rewarded and celebrated.

These examples demonstrate that in our society, the action is less significant than the context and intent of the action. Even when one reads scriptures and religious texts, one finds that for both piety and sin, action matters, but what matters more is the intent behind the action.

Someone may be forced to act piously, or be charitable, but if their heart is not in it, it amounts to nothing on the cosmic scale.

Similarly, an ordinarily abominable act like lying becomes a *dharmic* act when the intent is to save someone from danger.

We see a similar incident in the Mahabharata when Yogeshwarishwar, the Supreme Personality of Godhead Shri

Krishna, asks Yuddhisthira to lie on the battlefield of Kurukshetra.

Reading such tales shouldn't make us start looking for excuses if and when we lie. Rather, the lesson is to constantly examine our actions—even morally upright and so-called pious ones—to determine our intent behind the action.

I always say that we can cheat another, confound them, put on a mask, and pretend even to our own selves but we cannot pretend with the universal force or cheat nature. God is observing not just our actions but our intentions as well.

As the Supreme Lord, Bhagavan Shri Krishna says in the Bhagavad Gita (18.61):

ईश्वर: सर्वभूतानां हृद्देशेऽर्जुन तिष्ठति ।
भ्रामयन्सर्वभूतानि यन्त्रारूढानि मायया ॥

The Supreme Lord is present in each one's heart, O Arjuna. It is the Lord who empowers the activities of the human beings who are contained in a covering of matter.

Your Reflection

After reading about Devi Sita's decision and the Vedic perspective on intent, has your understanding of dharma shifted in any way? How can you apply the wisdom of intent-based action in your life to navigate ethical dilemmas with clarity and righteousness?

तिन्ह कर भय माता मोहि नाहीं । जौं तुम्ह सुख मानहु मन माहीं ॥

O Mother, I have no fear of these demons. If my words bring you even a little comfort, then I shall be satisfied.

Chapter 2

This Cannot be a Vanara's Work

नाथ एक आवा कपि भारी । तेहिं असोक बाटिका उजारी ॥
खाएसि फल अरु बिटप उपारे । रच्छक मर्दि मर्दि महि डारे ॥

When the bewildered guards and demonesses rushed to the palace to report that a Vanara was wreaking havoc in Ravana's gardens, the demon king initially dismissed their claims as drunken ramblings from the previous night's festivities.

For Ravana, who was fuelled by arrogance and disdain, the notion that mere humans or Vanaras—whom he considered vastly inferior—could disrupt his domain was ludicrous. After all, his prowess had subdued even the celestial *devatas*; what threat could earth dwellers pose?

Ravana's disdain for humans wasn't a new development. Even before acquiring his formidable powers and boons from the creator Brahma, he had exhibited a condescending attitude, neglecting to seek immunity against humans and Vanaras—a decision he might have regretted later.

Despite previous humiliations at the hands of humans and Vanaras, including being captured by the powerful human king

Kartyavira Arjuna and humbled by the Vanara king, Vali—who amusingly had him wrapped in his tail while traveling across Bharat—Ravana's pride had allowed him to conveniently forget these past defeats.

These episodes had not just been minor scuffles, but had proved to be significant blows to his ego.

(The humiliation at the hands of Vali was engineered by the mystical cosmic saint Narada Muni to rein in Ravana's ego.)

There is also a mention of Ravana once trying to conquer Shri Bali Maharaj, grandson of the great Vaishnava Shri Prahlad. Bali was protected by his deity Vamana, an avatar of Bhagavan Vishnu, and ordained the ruler of a heavenly nether world called Sutala. When Ravana tried to approach the kingdom and wage a battle against King Bali, he was kicked out of the realm by Vamana Bhagavan.

Yet, the idea that someone could infiltrate Lanka and cause such chaos seemed beyond belief to Ravana. He assumed it must be the work of the *devatas*, or perhaps even Bhagavan Shriman Narayan himself, for no lesser being could dare breach his formidable security.

Determined to quell what he considered a minor disturbance, Ravana dispatched 80,000 of his elite soldiers, the Kinkaras, to the Ashoka Grove, expecting them to easily subdue the intruder.

The confrontation that ensued was nothing short of epic. Shri Hanuman, on seeing the army, transformed into a colossal form, meeting their barrage of weapons with the ease of a child swatting away flies. His massive tail pounded the earth as he bellowed the chants:

Jai Shri Rama! Jai Shri Lakshmana!

He announced: 'My name is Hanuman, the son of Vayu and the servant of Shri Rama! What to speak of you all, not even a thousand Ravanas can withstand me.'

Hanuman's booming voice, gigantic size and form, struck terror in the hearts of the demons. Never before had they encountered such a powerful being!

Hanuman moved at a blistering pace and using an iron bar knocked the entire army out within a short span of time.

The readers who may be familiar with comic book movies like *Batman Begins*, can imagine Hanuman's swift takedown of the demons akin to Batman stealthily taking down gangsters. The difference here is that Hanuman didn't have to hide in the shadows to launch his attacks.

The surviving demons fled in terror, their reports sending Ravana into a state of incredulous fury. It was one thing to disrupt his garden, quite another to rout an army of 80,000.

Ravana summoned one of his most trusted generals—the constantly inebriated son of the Lankan minister Prahasta, Jambumali to tackle this onslaught.

Ravana briefed Jambumali that he had been summoned not to tackle the *devatas* but a Vanara this time.

Jambumali was taken aback considering it beneath himself to spar with puny beings such as Vanaras. But upon hearing that a mere Vanara had destroyed the Ashoka Grove and killed innumerable soldiers alone, Jambumali prepared himself for an exciting contest.

As Jambumali arrived, he launched a fierce verbal and physical attack on Hanuman.

Due to the relentless shooting by Jambumali, Shri Ramadoot was pierced by arrows all over his body. Although blood oozed out, it did not bother him. Rather, all the blood pouring out of his body made Shri Hanuman appear like a big, beautiful red lotus.

Shri Ramadoot sent trees and boulders in the direction of

the demon and his army, but all of it was countered easily by the skilful demon. After a bit of play at the demon's expense and having had enough of Jambumali's archery, Shri Ramadoot, decided to end the battle with the demon.

Hanuman picked up the iron bar once again, with which he had slain the *kinkara* soldiers. Jumping high into the air, he came down crashing both Jambumali's chariot and his evil existence.

Ravana couldn't believe his ears when he heard that Jambumali, who was a match to even the gods in military skills, was killed so effortlessly by a mere Vanara!

Seven more powerful and mighty warriors followed Jambumali to death. All these warriors were skilled in warfare, knew the use of celestial weapons, and had attacked Hanuman in unison. But all of them were effortlessly slain by the Rudra Avatar. The remaining members of the army fled in fear as Shri Vayuputra roared joyously.

'Ask Ravana to send more warriors; I will slay them all. I am the servant of Shri Rama, and my name is Hanuman. Soon millions of warriors like me will arrive along with Shri Rama and Lakshmana. If you and your warriors wish to live, then send Sita back to Shri Rama.'

Ravana felt the Vanara was now mocking him and his valour. But was it even a Vanara?

Never before had Ravana heard about or faced such a formidable personality.

Ravana was reminded of his trysts with various Vanara warriors in the past as well. Still, none ever seemed to be as powerful as Hanuman appeared to be.

The next batch of demons were Ravana's most formidable generals—Virupaksha, Yupaksha, Durdhara, Praghasa, and Bhaskarna. All these warriors had thus far been victorious in their individual conquests. Surely, the combined might of these warriors would prove to be too much for the insolent Vanara. Or so Ravana thought.

This time, Vayuputra didn't even allow some of the demon generals to put up a fight. Jumping from one chariot to another, he destroyed the first three warriors in a flash.

Praghasa and Bhaskarna managed to strike their weapons and draw blood, but that further incensed Mahavir Hanuman, and with a mere slap each, he disposed of the two warriors.

Unleashing his fiercest form, Hanuman made the most beautiful section of Lanka resemble a resting place for corpses. Mutilated bodies of the *rakshasa* warriors, broken chariots, and wheels filled the grove.

Imagine yourself as the king and leader of the most prosperous kingdom on the face of the planet. Knowing that you command an army that has previously been more than a match even for gods, you wouldn't, even in your wildest imagination, think some being would single-handedly destroy battalions of your military units. Not just ordinary soldiers, but skilled and armed men who were experts in the art of warfare were also demolished with ease. What would go through your mind? Seems quite inconceivable, right? And now imagine the personification of brute force, evil mindset, and ego, Ravana being humbled and humiliated like this!

To Ravana, this seemed like a prolonged nightmare. First, he woke up and heard some bitter words of admonition from Sita, then lost a significant number of army men who perished while failing to contain a lone Vanara. In this state of anxiety, and uncertainty, Ravana turned towards one of his dearest sons, Aksha Kumar.

Aksha Kumar resembled Ravana in every aspect—his gait,

form, and even skills were of the highest order. Defeat was not something that Aksha ever had to encounter in his life. This was as safe a bet as Ravana could make in a warlike situation.

Surely, Aksha could overcome this Vanara. Or could he?

Key Takeaway
Know that Everything is Ephemeral
Continuing our learnings from this section and previous chapters, Hanuman's humbling and humiliation of the egoistic demons is a lesson to never be complacent.

The Universe, Gods, and the higher powers have the most unique and unexpected ways of humbling us.

Our abilities, our powers, and our elevated positions are gifts from God; a wise person knows them to be temporary.

What history effectively teaches us is that no matter how powerful you end up becoming via your pious karmas, if you fail to cultivate qualities of humility, someday you'll be in for a rude reality check.

Remember, nothing in this world is permanent—not your name, fame, power, or glory. They can all vanish in an instant. The star of today may not even make tomorrow's news. This is the transient nature of our world, a reminder of the importance of humility and service.

Ramayana teaches us that powers are a gift, and their value is in service, not in boasting and subjugating other beings.

We should never mistake humility for lack of ability or self-deprecation. You may not find any other being as humble as Hanuman. But as we can see in our story, he never shied away from displaying his might when needed.

Additionally, Shri Vayuputra never considered himself to be the sole proprietor of his powers and abilities. He always used his abilities to serve others.

Humility lies in recognising that we are not the sole cause of our talents, abilities, and successes.

Your Reflection
Define what humility means to you.

सुनि रावन पठए भट नाना । तिन्हहि देखि गर्जेउ हनुमाना ॥ सब रजनीचर कपि संघारे । गए पुकारत कछु अधमारे ॥

Ravana sent a number of soldiers, who encountered the mighty roars of Hanuman. All the demons were vanquished by him and some who were still half-alive, ran away crying from the battle with the giant Vanara.

Chapter 3

Restrain Him By Any Means Possible

Aksha, a radiant young demon brimming with the vigour of youth, was among Ravana's most cherished sons. Having mastered martial arts early on, his presence on the battlefield, aboard a regal chariot escorted by an elite cadre of soldiers, drew Shri Hanuman's gaze. In Aksha, Maruti noted a resemblance not just in appearance, but in the fierce resolve that mirrored Ravana, himself.

Maruti pondered the depths of the demon king's obsession, willing to sacrifice his own flesh and blood in a futile quest for Sita's captivity. It was a testament to a blinding desire that clouded every judgement.

On the battlefield, Aksha was struck with awe at the formidable sight of the great Vanara. Despite his mastery over the dark arts, the young demon found himself overwhelmed by the divine aura of Shri Ramadoot. With youthful brashness, he unleashed his arsenal, launching his most formidable weapons at Maruti, hoping to overpower him.

But Vayuputra, moving with the swiftness of the wind, dodged every attack with ease. In a display of unmatched prowess, he leapt onto Aksha's chariot, shattering it into splinters with his mere presence. As the chariot lay in ruins, Aksha ascended, propelled by his mystical powers, only to be caught by Hanuman.

With a swift motion, Shri Ramadoot spun the young demon high above before decisively smashing him into the earth, ending the tragic trajectory of Ravana's son.

The celestial audience above, witnessing this monumental duel, were left astounded by Hanuman's valour. They cascaded heavenly flowers upon him, celebrating the downfall of a formidable adversary.

The news of Aksha's demise sent shockwaves through Lanka, numbing Ravana to his core. His kingdom had lost not just a quarter-million warriors in mere hours, but now, a beloved son lay vanquished. The gravity of the situation was palpable—Lanka was on the brink of despair.

In this dire hour, Ravana turned to his mightiest warrior and dearest son, Meghnada, known also as Indrajit for his celestial prowess and past victory over the king of heaven.

With a heavy heart laden with vengeance and despair, Ravana briefed his son. The mission was clear—subdue the Vanara that no ordinary soldier could contend with.

Indrajit, riding his mystical chariot drawn by four fierce lions, approached the battlefield with a storm of arrows aimed at Hanuman. Yet, each missile was artfully dodged by the nimble Maruti, who seemed both untouchable and invincible.

Recognising the extraordinary challenge at hand, Indrajit resorted to the ultimate celestial weapon—the *Brahmastra*. Chanting sacred mantras, he invoked the divine energy of the creator, launching the potent arrow towards Hanuman.

ब्रह्म अस्त्र तेहि साँधा कपि मन कीन्ह बिचार । जौं न ब्रह्मसर मानउँ महिमा मिटइ अपार ॥

In that critical moment, Hanuman, aware of the blessings bestowed upon him in his youth that granted him immunity against the weapon, chose to honour the *Brahmastra's* sanctity.

He bowed in reverence to the creator's weapon, acknowledging the immense power it wielded. Though capable of resisting its impact, out of respect for the creator and to demonstrate humility, Anjaneya allowed himself to be bound by the weapon, transformed into ethereal ropes.

This apparent capture sparked jubilation among the Lankan forces, yet Indrajit experienced a moment of frustration as his warriors, unaware of the *Brahmastra's* unique properties, hastily bound Shri Hanuman with additional ropes, unwittingly nullifying its effects.

Despite the humiliation, Shri Ramadoot displayed an inner smile. He knew his purpose here and while it seemed to the Lankan soldiers that they had captured the Vanara and were dragging him towards the court, in actuality, it was Hanuman's independent will that was taking him to Ravana.

What happens when the messenger of Shri Rama meets the king of Lanka?

What happens when the embodiment of ego meets the personification of an ego-less existence?

What happens when the embodiment of lust meets the legendary celibate?

What happens when the selfish meets the selfless?

We continue to weave through the epic tapestry of the Ramayana, exploring the depths of devotion and the strength of spirit over sheer might.

Key Takeaway
Learning to be Adaptable

Imagine being one of the most powerful beings to have ever existed and then to endure such a humiliating situation! But that is how an ordinary person's ego would perceive the situation. For Shri Ramadoot, every situation in his life was just an opportunity to be of some use and service to someone.

It is not a fluke or some engineered PR campaign that has made Hanuman one of the most beloved deities of Vedic Sanatana Dharma. Hanuman's greatness lies in functioning from an ego-less state. There is nothing for him to achieve on a personal level—no reward that he seeks, no position, no recognition; Maruti's entire existence is about serving people, about bringing joy, peace, and harmony. A personality that functions with such an attitude would inevitably gain legendary status.

Arguably, it may be easy for someone who has not worked on their talent and ability, or acquired blessings to function from an ego-less state. But it is quite astonishing when someone like Hanuman who is the embodiment of strength, valour and intelligence chooses to remain so grounded and free from the trap of the ego. Hanuman exemplifies the Sanskrit verse:

विद्या ददाति विनयं, विनयाद्याति पात्रताम् ।

True knowledge grants one humility, humility makes one eligible for blessings. Also, as we keep advancing in life, (usually) our goals and definition of success keep evolving and changing.

Lord Hanuman started his journey to locate Sita. He went through countless trials, overcame distractions, obstacles, despondency, and self-doubt to finally reach Devi Sita. He attained her blessings, gave her hope, and fulfilled his mission. Then, he got another idea of what would truly constitute success.

As we keep advancing, we should keep growing, and keep space for adaptability, for change, and spontaneity.

Your Reflection
Has there ever been a time when you had to compromise or adapt to ensure you remained on course for success?

जासु नाम जपि सुनहु भवानी । भव बंधन काटहिं नर ग्यानी ॥ तासु दूत कि बंध तरु आवा । प्रभु कारज लगि कपिहिं बँधावा ॥

Lord Shiva said, O dear Parvati, chanting whose names can cut the ties of repeated birth and death, could His messenger ever be captured? It was only to serve his master that Hanuman allowed himself to be caught.

Chapter 4

I'm an Ordinary Vanara

अहो रूपमहो धैर्यमहोत्सवमहो द्युति: ।
अहो राक्षसराजस्य सर्वलक्षणयुक्तता ॥

> 'What form! What fortitude! What valour! What splendour!
> He is indeed not inferior to the gods, nor the Gandharvas, nor the Asuras, nor the Rakshasas.'
> (*Valmiki Ramayana, Sundara Kanda*, 49.17)

As Shri Hanuman was brought before the demon king, the hallowed court of Lanka fell silent. Amidst the hostile stares and the charged atmosphere, Vayuputra gazed up, absorbing the formidable aura of Ravana, whose presence had threatened the tranquillity of the celestial realms.

'Had the king of demons fostered a noble heart, he might have been revered as the guardian of even the celestial worlds,' Hanuman mused.

His saintly demeanour allowed him to perceive potential goodness even in the darkest of souls. This introspective moment reflects the profound grace and wisdom of Shri Ramadoot, who, despite the circumstances, maintained a serene command over his emotions—a true marker of his greatness.

Amidst the simmering tensions, cries for vengeance filled the court—'Kill him, burn him, roast him!' echoed the enraged assembly.

Yet, Ravana, his heart scorched by the loss of his son and his army, chose first to probe the identity of the mighty Vanara who had so captivated his attention.

As Mahavir Hanuman stood resolute before Ravana, the demon king's thoughts drifted to a dark chapter of his past—a sequence of transgressions that had sealed his fate through divine curses.

Years ago, having vanquished the celestial realms, Ravana usurped the mystical Pushpak Vimana from his cousin Kubera. With this celestial chariot, he and his minions would often disrupt the serenity of sages and yogis absorbed in deep meditation across secluded forests and mountainsides.

It was on one such intrusive flight that Ravana encountered the ascetic Vedavati. Her formidable spiritual presence daunted even the mighty Ravana. When his attempts to abduct her were thwarted, Vedavati sacrificed her physical form and uttered a curse—foretelling that her spirit would become the harbinger of Ravana's destruction in a future birth.

Another fateful incident unfolded as Ravana, aboard the Pushpak, soared over the sacred Kailasa mountain—the hallowed abode of Lord Shiva. Suddenly, the chariot faltered and ground to a halt.

As it descended, Ravana found himself under the stern gaze of a formidable figure. Nandi, the celestial gatekeeper and devout attendant of Mahadeva, who bore the head of a Vanara and wielding a pike, blocked his path. With a voice resonating with divine authority, Nandi declared, 'Kailasa is the sacred abode of Bhagavan Shiva. It is sanctified ground, forbidden to mortals. Depart at once.'

Amused by Nandi's vanara-like appearance and intoxicated by his conquests, Ravana mocked the divine sentinel, scoffing at the sacred decrees of Lord Shiva.

In response to this affront, Nandi pronounced a curse: 'You scorn my vanara form, yet it will be vanaras who will humble you, heralding the downfall of you and your lineage.'

Incensed and dismissive of the divine power, Ravana boastfully attempted to upheave Mount Kailasa itself—a reckless act of defiance. His audacity provoked Ma Parvati, who, disturbed by his arrogance, cursed Ravana to meet his end through the machinations of a woman.

To pacify His divine consort, Sarveshwar Shiva stood up and firmly pressed down the toe of his foot on the mountain. As Ravana strained under the mountain, his hubris crushed by Shiva's mere toe, cries of pain echoed through the cosmos. Advised by his minions, Ravana composed poetry and hymns to propitiate the compassionate Mahadev.

Shiva, known for his swift forgiveness, eventually appeared, alleviating Ravana's torment. Yet, in a display of unabashed temerity, Ravana beseeched Shiva for the fearsome Pashupatastra, a boon granted by the merciful deity.

These recollections were interrupted as he gazed upon Hanuman, brought forth in chains yet undeterred in spirit. His ministers, stirred by the presence of the formidable Vanara, inquired about his origins and motives.

Prahasta, a prominent minister and the father of the slain Jambumali, enquired:

'Who are you, O Vanara? Be truthful, and we may spare your life. Are you an envoy of Vishnu, the prime enemy of our race? You appear to be a Vanara, but your strength belies that. Has *Indra, Kubera, Varuna, Yama,* or any of the gods sent you here? Why did you destroy the Ashoka Grove and killed so many of our warriors?'

Though being addressed by Prahasta, Shri Hanuman spoke directly to the demon king:

'I am neither an envoy of the *devatas* nor Bhagavan Shri Vishnu. I am simply an ordinary Vanara. It is quite a task to get an audience with the king. I destroyed the grove and the *rakshasas*, hoping to get a word with the king. I am the son of Vayu, and my name is Hanuman. Let it be known that I have been given immunity from all kinds of weapons and nooses by the boon of the creator, Brahma. The effect of the weapon has already subsided, and I am here only to deliver the message of my Lord, proprietor of unlimited splendour, Shri Rama!'

This declaration sent ripples through the court. Hanuman continued to recount the valiant efforts of the Vanara army led by King Sugreeva, emphasising the grave error Ravana had made by abducting Ma Sita. With resonant clarity, he warned of the dire consequences should Ravana fail to return her to Shri Rama.

Shri Ramadoot reminded Ravana that he had acquired his fame, riches, power, and wealth through the practice of austerities. By abducting another man's wife, he had committed a huge error. If he did not restore Ma Sita swiftly back to the mighty Raghuveer, Ravana and his hordes of demons would surely be annihilated.

'The daughter of Janaka is a form of Kalarathri (Goddess of death and destruction) right now for you, Lankesh and your Lanka. Devi Sita cannot be overpowered by you any more than a person can digest poison and live to tell the story.'

The court was left in stunned silence, for never before had they witnessed such fearless candour. The audacity of Lord Hanuman, to proclaim his voluntary bondage, was beyond their comprehension.

In a final plea, Vayuputra appealed to Ravana's dwindling sense of reason, urging him to rectify his grievous mistake for the sake of his people and his legacy. He boldly declared Shri Rama's divine prowess, unmatched even by the gods, and capable of obliterating and reshaping worlds.

सर्वान् लोकान् सुसंहृत्य सभूतान् सचराचरान् पुनरेव तथा स्रष्टुं शक्तो रामो महायशाः

'The renowned Rama is capable of totally destroying all the worlds together with its five elements, along with its animate and inanimate things, and also to create yet again all the worlds in like manner as before.'
(Valmiki Ramayan, Sundar Kand, 51.39)

Even the army of *devas* is incapable of withstanding Rama in battle, O Ravana. His valour is as mighty as that of Shri Narayan. None can stay safe and secure if they dare cause an affront to Rama. Even Brahma or Tripurari Shri Shiva cannot protect the one ordained to be killed by Shri Rama.

Hanuman's message was clear—surrender or be vanquished from the face of the earth.

As Ravana's fury reached its peak, he could no longer tolerate the Vanara's discourse. Overcome by rage, he ordered Hanuman's immediate execution. Yet, as the guards advanced, a commanding voice halted their charge:

'STOP!'

Who dared to challenge the tyrant's wrath?

Key Takeaway
What We Give Out Comes Back

In this chapter, we briefly discussed an incident from Ravana's past—a curse that seemed to have manifested in front of him in the form of Shri Ramadoot.

When we read Vedic scriptures, we find numerous stories of curses and blessings; some curses turning into blessings and blessings transforming into a curse.

These stories teach us that no action goes unaccounted for. From the smallest to the most significant of our acts, there is a consequence. The consequence may either be one that helps us, aids us, one that can teach us, transform us, or punish us—all of it is dependent upon our response to each situation.

For instance, Ravana's blessing of immeasurable strength from Brahma turned into a curse not just for the world but also for himself because his unbridled power led him to accrue numerous curses, and sins, and these ultimately led to his downfall.

Additionally, what we can learn and pick from such stories is the realisation that words have tremendous power, specially when uttered in an intense state of mind and presence. Words we utter toward others and especially the words we speak to ourselves, must always be **conscious**. Words, thoughts, and emotions can all have a strong interlink.

It is not that one needs to be a saint, a being of a higher realm, or a part of an epic to pronounce a blessing or a curse. We, too, in our own small little way can experiment by blessing ourselves and those around us with words of kindness, love and abundance. Because what we give out always comes back.

And in the unlikely scenario that you may end up attracting any sort of negativity despite vibrating at a higher level of awareness, know that even a curse will turn into a blessing for you if you are consciously connected to God.

Your Reflection

What are the words that you need to hear right now?

If you were to ask for a blessing, what would it be?

जाके बल लवलेस तें जितेहु चराचर झारि । तासु दूत मैं जा करि हरि आनेहु प्रिय नारि ॥

By the dint of whose power you became a universal conquerer and whose wife you abducted, I am the messenger of that Lord.

Chapter 5

Don't Shoot the Messenger

नाइ सीस करि बिनय बहूता । नीति बिरोध न मारिअ दूता ॥

Vibhishana, the noble outlier among demons, stood resolute in his virtue amidst the court of Lanka. As Ravana's younger brother, he upheld the sage-like wisdom and moral integrity often uncharacteristic of their race. With a measured voice, he interjected, guided by ancient political codes:

'A messenger should never be slain, my lord. While you may injure, maim, or even humiliate him, the death of a Vanara who serves merely as a messenger would tarnish an illustrious king's reputation. Rather, let the lesson be for the master who sent him.'

Ravana, incensed by Hanuman's audacity—his destruction of the sacred grove, the slaying of thousands, and his bold insults in open court—nonetheless recognised his brother's astute grasp of diplomacy.

The notion of tormenting the Vanara, perhaps even parading him through the streets of Lanka, sparked a cruel delight. It could serve as a spectacle, soothing the citizens' rattled spirits.

'The tail,' declared Ravana, fixating on the pride of every Vanara, 'set it ablaze. Should he survive, let him return, a scorned reminder of his folly.'

On Ravana's grim decree, soldiers scrambled, collecting oil-soaked rags, attempting to wrap Hanuman's ever-lengthening tail. The scripture poignantly captures this scene:

रहा न नगर बसन घृत तेला। बाढ़ी पूँछ कीन्ह कपि खेला।।

Tulsidas narrates how Shri Hanuman, in playful defiance, extended his tail endlessly, draining the city of its resources.

As he was paraded, jeered, and tormented, the clever Shri Ramadoot, Hanuman, observed every alley and fortification of Lanka—a strategic reconnaissance for the impending battle. Yet, as flames engulfed his tail, a divine anomaly occurred. Agni Dev, the deity of fire, transformed his scorching touch into a soothing caress—a miracle of faith bearing the fingerprints of divine intervention.

Meanwhile, secluded in her captivity, Bhagavati Sita received word of Hanuman's plight. Her heart, already heavy, sank further. Viewing Hanuman as a son, she could not bear the thought of his suffering for her sake. In a moment of profound spiritual fervour, she invoked her unwavering devotion to Rama: 'If my devotion is pure, let this fire cool him rather than consume.'

The blaze that should have tormented him felt cool, a serene blessing directly bestowed by Bhagavati Sita's prayer. Recognising this divine intervention, Hanuman paid inward homage to his revered protector, energised by the divine mother's grace.

With renewed spirit and a mischievous glint in his eye, Hanuman now prepared to turn his harrowing ordeal into a tactical triumph. His plan, as audacious as it was mischievous, would unfold in the heart of Lanka.

Key Takeaway
Count Your Blessings, Always!

Sita's power must be acknowledged and noted. She makes even fire give a cooling sensation to Hanuman! If she so desired, she could burn down not just Ravana, but his entire kingdom by the dint of her yogic powers. Sita is no ordinary damsel in distress.

We understand from scriptures, Vedic scholars, and saints that when the divine descends among us in human form or any other form for that matter, they engage in what is called *Lila* or play. As part of that play, it may appear that they are in distress. But time and again in the *play*, we witness them performing miraculous things, revealing their divinity or power.

Another essential thing to note, which I keep harping upon repeatedly in the book is the power of blessings. Shri Hanuman, whose life is all about receiving blessings and offering service to others, is a prime example that success requires blessings.

We may not be fortunate enough to 'directly' receive blessings from a divine personality like in the case of Lord Hanuman but we should never discount the blessings received through elders, family, friends, or even strangers. The power imbued in heartfelt blessings received from any person, even an animal, can transform an individual's life.

Our lesson here is to live a life that is a 'blessing attractor'—our service, intentions and acts towards life and people around should be such that blessings pour out to us from others.

A very important addition to this idea is to also offer blessings to anyone and everyone we encounter. This, in itself, can be an effective *sadhna*. The universal laws are such that you receive what you give out. It may sound deceptively simple, but once experimented with, you would know it to be true:

Want love, then start offering more love to others.

Want respect, then start offering more respect to others.

Want blessings…you know the drill....

Your Reflection

As part of your reflection, recall a time when you received a blessing from someone, perhaps an elder, a relative, friend, saint or even a stranger. How did it make you feel? What is that one blessing you would wish to receive for your life journey, and which is that one blessing you may wish to offer to others?

ता कर दूत अनल जेहिं सिरिजा । जरा न सो तेहि कारन गिरिजा ॥

O Girija (Parvati Ma), Hanuman is the messenger of that very Lord (Shri Rama), who created fire itself. How could fire ever burn him?

Chapter 6

Everything Burns

जिन्ह कै कीन्हिसि बहुत बड़ाई । देखउँ मैं तिन्ह कै प्रभुताई ।।

Goswami Tulsidas describes how Ravana, in his disdain, mocked Hanuman before commanding his minions to set his tail ablaze.

'Let us witness the divine prowess of the master this Vanara extols,' sneered Ravana.

Amidst the mockery, Shri Ramadoot offered a serene smile, offering gratitude to Ma Saraswati, the goddess of speech and learning, for inspiring the right words from Ravana.

As Maruti surveyed the pompous city of Lanka, he realised it was time to illuminate the darkness of ignorance with a divine fire. Lanka, a bastion of tyranny and unchecked dominion, was about to experience a celestial upheaval—a seismic jolt to Ravana's pride they would never erase from memory.

Shrinking to elude his bonds, Shri Ramadoot sprang into the air. As he chanted Bhagavan Shri Rama's sacred name, he leaped across rooftops and ramparts, igniting them with the fiery banner of his tail.

'Jai Shri Rama, Jai Shri Rama, Jai Shri Rama!' he chanted.

The battle cry of Shri Ramadoot echoed through the expanses of Lanka, heralding a mission to humble the vainglorious demons.

Aided by Agni Dev and his father Vayu, who conjured 49 celestial winds to amplify His son's fury, Vajrangi, in His colossal, mountainous form, swiftly engulfed the golden city in a conflagration.

Unsuspecting demons, who had revelled in tormenting Maruti just moments before, now scrambled in terror. Those who had mocked and assaulted him were now flailing in despair, realising too late the unstoppable force of the Vanara. Even Lanka's most revered warriors, famed for their valour, found themselves powerless against the whirlwind fury of Vayuputra.

Demons plunged into water bodies to escape the scorching blaze, while others sought refuge in the vast ocean, their only sanctuary. The once invincible Lanka was now a tableau of chaos—how swiftly fortunes turn!

'It must be the great Indra!'
'Surely, it's Agni unleashing his fury upon us and our king.'
'No, this can only be Lord Shiva performing his Tandav!'
'Or perhaps, the Supreme Lord Vishnu Himself is manifest here.'

Amidst the turmoil, whispers of divine intervention spread like wildfire among the astonished citizens. The once-dismissed legends of the Vanara's celestial origin were now vividly confirmed by the apocalyptic scenes unfolding before their eyes.

'If such is the might of the servant, imagine the omnipotence of the master!'

Mahavir Hanuman's strategic devastation sowed seeds of dread, uncertainty, and fear in the hearts of Lanka's denizens.

Ravana, whose arrogance had once seemed unshakeable, was

now compelled to confront the consequences of his transgressions against Sita Devi and Shri Rama. Perhaps, just perhaps, he would reconsider his ruinous path and seek reconciliation with the compassionate Raghuveer.

In his towering form, Mahaveer surveyed the ashes of what was once a majestic city. In just moments, he had reduced it to cinders. Such is the fleeting nature of material existence, where certainty is but an illusion.

Remarkably, Vibhishana's house remained untouched by the flames. Even the fire deity, like Shri Hanuman, recognised the purity of Vibhishana's soul. Grateful for Vibhishana's advocacy in Ravana's court, Maruti acknowledged the solitary voice of *dharma* amidst the corrupt echelons of Lanka.

As celestial beings who had long suffered under Ravana's tyranny watched, they found deep satisfaction in the unfolding justice. They rained down fragrant flowers upon Hanuman, lauding his wisdom, courage, and valour.

But amidst the victory and valour, a sudden realisation dimmed Shri Ramadoot's exultation. In the heat of his righteous wrath, had he jeopardised Ma Sita's safety?

The thought struck Him like a thunderbolt.

How would he face Shri Rama, Sugreeva, and his companions? Had his anger inadvertently led to an unfathomable disaster?

Key Takeaway
Be Forever Mindful and Conscious

Shri Hanuman had to endure a lot of brickbats—literally, as he was bound by ordinary demons and citizens. Of course, they were releasing their angst against the mighty Maruti, who had caused such immense damage to them. But in our context, we can equate this to enduring criticism, brickbats, and insults one has to endure on the path to success.

We know Lord Hanuman was more than capable of responding back to the demons. He could have clobbered them in a moment's time if he so wanted. After all, he was only pretending to be bound up. But Shri Ramadoot endured, keeping his composure and ultimately wreaked havoc on the demons.

In our case, we can learn that success requires us to keep a calm head. If we keep expanding our energy towards random things, we will lose sight of our goal. Shri Hanuman kept up his act of being bound and endured the humiliation because he was focused on his goal of scanning all the militarily critical locations of Lanka.

It is often compelling to respond back, give it back, or demonstrate one's prowess when people try to throw negativity towards us. But internally chanting the names of God and never losing sight of the goal ultimately leads us to success.

Second, we see how Hanuman is overcome with regret and worry after his demonstration of anger and power. Maruti was concerned the fire might have burned Devi Sita as well. While his act was not one committed out of ego or for displaying his extraordinary might, this incident teaches us how anger, if left unchecked, may cause damage even to the things dear to us. Yogeshwar Bhagavan Shri Krishna says it beautifully in the Bhagavad Gita:

क्रोधाद्भवति सम्मोहः सम्मोहात्स्मृतिविभ्रमः।
स्मृतिभ्रंशाद्बुद्धिनाशो बुद्धिनाशात्प्रणश्यति ॥

'From anger arises illusion; illusion leads to loss of memory. Loss of memory leads to destruction of intelligence and once one's intelligence is destroyed, the person is led towards destruction.'

There is a really apt saying in Hindi, as well:

सावधानी हटी दुर्घटना घटी

In other words, even in a positive state of euphoria, one should endeavour to be mindful and conscious. Even a single moment and act of recklessness can lead to destruction of our success.

Yes, I hear you, dear reader. Anger is not something that is easy to curb. It is also not healthy to suppress it artificially. The message I am trying to put out, essentially based upon my personal life experiences and life around is that anger must be channelled, not suppressed.

Anger is the natural state of human expression when we feel threatened or someone intrudes into our personal space. Shri

Hanuman teaches us both to channelise anger and express it at the most appropriate moment and cause. And importantly, remember not to lose awareness of the potential destruction it can cause.

Your Reflection
What is your story? How do you manage your temper, and what lessons have you derived from your life and by observing others on channeling anger?

हरि प्रेरित तेहि अवसर चले मरुत उनचास । अट्टहास करि गर्जा कपि बढ़ि लाग अकास ॥

Inspired by Lord Hari (Shri Rama), at that very moment, the forty-nine Wind Gods moved. Lord Hanuman roared with a mighty laugh and, increasing in size, leaped into the sky.

Chapter 7

See You Soon, Ma

When Hanuman was floating in a sea of despondency, the celestial bards who were witnessing the satiating sight of their oppressor's palace being burned down announced:

'Hanuman has fulfilled a really difficult task of burning down Ravana's Lanka. Even as it has caused tremendous agony to the demons and even though the city markets, ramparts, archways and doorways were burned, Devi Sita remains unscathed.'

This news filled Shri Ramadoot with immense delight and relief. He reasoned, 'By whose grace fire could not touch me, how could it harm that divine personality?'

Vayuputra then sought Ma Sita's blessings once more before his departure from Lanka.

पूँछ बुझाइ खोइ श्रम धरि लघु रूप बहोरि । जनकसुता के आगें ठाढ़ भयउ कर जोरि ॥

Resuming his diminutive form, Maruti landed gracefully in Ashoka Vatika, bowing deeply before Devi Sita. His heart swelled with gratitude for her divine protection and joy at her safety.

Sita's face lit up with a radiant smile as she bestowed her blessings on her son once more. She acknowledged the temptation to leave with him at that very moment, but her unwavering determination to wait for Rama to personally vanquish the demon king was evident in her words.

Amidst mixed emotions of hope, joy, and imminent separation, Sita reinforced the urgency of the one-month deadline, urging Hanuman to hasten Rama's arrival.

Shri Ramadoot, with calming assurances of Lord Rama's imminent victory, promised that the forces of good would soon converge on Lanka to end the demonic reign. After offering his reverent *pranam* to Devi Sita, Vayuputra leapt toward *Arishta* mountain. Transforming into a colossal form, he roared mightily:

Jai Shri Ram!
His mighty leap caused Arishta mountain to tremble and sink back into the earth, while the demons, consumed by fear and confusion, dared not pursue.

Ravana's palace was spared by Agni out of fear of the ferocious and powerful demon. However, Ravana was overcome with doubts and worry as he witnessed his great city burned down.

Once again, Brahma's boon and the lack of immunity from humans (and vanaras) came to his mind.

Was Rama really an incarnation of Vishnu?

Would Rama prove to be his downfall?

No matter what, Ravana was adamant that he would not let go of Sita. Rama would have to fight and go through him and his army if he wanted her back.

Lord Hanuman, speeding back across the ocean, was soon a majestic sight in the skies, his form heralding success to the awaiting Vanaras. On his heroic return to Mount Mahendra, he was greeted with jubilant cheers and roars from the Vanara warriors. Under the leadership of Angad and the sagely Jambavan, they honoured him with garlands and offerings, celebrating the successful mission.

Prince Angad was bursting with excitement to know the details of Maruti's journey to Lanka. Shri Hanuman lovingly held his hand and narrated the events of the past two days to the eager audience.

The Vanaras were awed as they heard about Hanuman's flight to Lanka. They praised his valour, intelligence and wit for entering Lanka.

They shed tears of agony and pain upon hearing the plight of Ma Janaki.

Anger boiled up in their hearts against Ravana and his ilk as they heard about his arrogant ways.

Angad was in no mood to retreat now. He called upon his warriors to leap across to Lanka and finish this menace of Ravana. How can they allow Ma Janaki to remain captive any longer?

The wise old bear, King Jambavan, though, poured cold water on the energetic prince's plan.

'Our duty was to find Ma Sita and report it back to King Sugreeva and Shri Rama. We must stick to the plan. Furthermore, as Anjaneya has said, it is Devi Sita's wish for Shri Rama to annihilate the demoniac Ravana, and we must honour her will.'

All the Vanaras nodded in agreement to the words of wisdom of the sagacious old bear. Their spirits soaring, hearts filled with excitement and hope, the Vanaras led by Angad, Jambavan, and Hanuman, started their journey back to Kishkindha—back to Lord Rama.

What happens whey they reach Kishkindha? What is Sugreeva's response, and how does the legendary meeting between Lord Rama and Shri Ramadoot pan out?

Key Takeaway
It's Never too Late to Learn

We see here that even a demoniac entity like Ravana hears the voice of intuition. He chose to ignore it but Paramatma within everyone's heart is the ultimate well wisher. He reaches out to warn us about the consequences of our actions. The voice of intuition is soft and firm, unlike the shrill voice of the mind and thoughts.

Ravana does seem to realise that Lord Rama may be the end of him, but his arrogance and ego are such that he isn't willing to bend.

What we can also learn from this is that God keeps granting us chances to mend our ways and improve upon our mistakes. As is said, it is never too late to learn or improve upon a mistake. The choice is always ours. There is no shame in admitting or even committing a mistake (missed-take). But the question is, can we learn from it?

As always, the humility and gracefulness of Shri Hanuman is always worth meditating upon.

He has achieved the impossible.

He has infused life in so many souls with his act.

He has ensured that the search party will gain credit and merit from the king and Shri Rama.

And yet, he remains magnificently humble. Success didn't change him, even if it (positively) changed so many things for other people around him. Hanuman still acts like a fellow soldier or minister in Sugreeva's army and he continued to do so until the very end.

Enduring success, as we have discussed often in our journey, is inevitably and invariably accompanied by humility.

Your Reflection

Everyone likes attention, even if we do not admit it. Here, I am talking about healthy attention, not the creepy, discomforting kind. It is one thing to receive adulation, love, and gratitude and quite another, to offer them to someone.

Think of a time in your life journey when you felt ecstatic at another's achievement. And here I am not talking about a sporting or some movie star, no. Someone you know personally, an equal, a friend or colleague. Next, reflect on what constitutes support for you and how you prefer to express it.

हरषे सब बिलोकि हनुमाना । नूतन जन्म कपिन्ह तब जाना ॥

All the vanaras were overjoyed looking at Hanuman. It seemed as if they had attained a new birth!

Section 5

The Messenger Gets Promoted

Chapter 1

Party Mode On

The search party triumphantly returned to Kishkindha within two days—a stark contrast to the two months it had taken them initially, as they had combed every nook and corner en route. Now, with Maruti's victory fuelling their spirits, each Vanara was brimming with excitement, eager to share their success story with King Sugreeva and Shri Rama.

On reaching Kishkindha, Angad led them directly into Sugreeva's private garden. For a fleeting moment, the Vanara warriors shed their residual fears and hesitations, delighting in the succulent fruits and the intoxicating nectar of the royal garden.

Dadhimukha, the vigilant guardian of *Madhuvan*, Sugreeva's prized garden, was taken aback by the audacity displayed by the Vanaras. It was unprecedented for anyone to breach the sanctity of the king's garden. His mind swirled with confusion and indignation. As a dutiful guard, Dadhimukha attempted to intervene and halt the Vanaras' revelry. However, led by the spirited Angad, the hapless Dadhimukha was playfully overpowered and ousted from the garden.

Out of breath and flustered, Dadhimukha hurried to report the unruly scene to the king.

'The prince and his search party are ravaging the grove, O King. Your intervention is required,' he pleaded.

To Dadhimukha's bewilderment, Sugreeva responded with a robust laugh.

Sugreeva, well-acquainted with his warriors' valour and wisdom, had been awaiting such news. He was confident that the southern search party, comprised of some of his most capable warriors, would not return without fulfilling their mission. He reasoned that they would not dare face him or even enter Madhuvan had they not succeeded.

'Let them enjoy all the fruits and honey they desire, Dadhimukha,' declared the elated king. 'Summon Angad and his companions to join me, along with Shri Rama and Lakshmana, atop Mount Malyavanta for an audience.'

Reassured by the king's jubilant demeanour, Dadhimukha returned to the grove, this time with respect and without fear, to relay the king's summons to the prince. Realising their time of leisure had ended, Angad promptly gathered his troops, informing them of their next assembly on Mount Malyavanta.

The return of Angad's party was a beacon of hope amidst the anxiety that had gripped Sugreeva, and even more so, Lord Rama and Lakshmana, whose hearts had grown heavy as each day stretched on like an eternity.

Informed of the party's arrival, Lakshmana and Sugreeva hastened towards their revered Lord Shri Rama, who had been cloaked in silent sorrow in recent months. Shri Ramadoot ascended the mountain, bearing the news his master so desperately yearned to hear. The sagacious Maruti would reveal this news in an unorthodox manner, bending the rules of language itself.

Key Takeaway
Leadership Lessons: A Balance of Play & Work

I was most positively fascinated on reading this section of the Ramayana. The Vanara search party had had an arduous but ultimately fulfilling journey. They knew a gruesome war was ahead. Now, as they were back home, they engaged in some well-deserved merry-making. It wasn't just about achieving the ultimate goal of rescuing Devi Sita. What I gleaned from this is the importance of being playful and celebrating the smaller victories along the way. This not only keeps us motivated but also encourages us to keep pushing forward.

Do not wait until you achieve your ultimate desire to celebrate. Additionally, balancing work with adequate breaks helps one retain healthy levels of focus. One must also appreciate Sugreeva and draw lessons in leadership from him. Leadership is about managing work load, tempering the need for obedience with freedom, and allowing some much needed playtime.

What to say of sentient beings, even machines need downtime. The culture of constant hustle only brings down the quality of work and leads to burnout. Sugreeva laughs rather than getting angry at his soldier's audacity of infiltrating his grove, knowing they deserve this fun time after all the hard work of the past few months.

Leadership can be a tricky path to tread. Sugreeva had sent out a stern warning to his soldiers to ensure they did their work sincerely. No wonder, at the beginning of our story and journey, the search party led by Angad feared going back. But Sugreeva delicately balances instilling discipline and order by ensuring that his soldiers deservedly get a party upon completing the task!

Your Reflection

How important is fun and play for your life? How do you like to celebrate your achievements? Recall a moment when you worked really hard for something and attained it. Did you celebrate that?

If not, let us plan on doing so now. It is never too late.

तब मधुबन भीतर सब आए । अंगद संमत मधु फल खाए ॥ रखवारे जब बरजन लागे । मुष्टि प्रहार हनत सब भागे ॥

They entered Madhuvan on Angad's cue and started eating fruits and drinking honey. When the guards intervened, they were chased away.

Chapter 2
Life Saviour Hanuman

With profound reverence, I invoke the immortal verses of Maharishi Valmiki, who has immortalised Bhagavan Rama's divine countenance. In humble homage, I strive to capture the majestic appearance of Paramatma Shri Rama in my own words.

Rama's arms, long and sturdy, reached down to his knees. His broad chest echoed the strength of his resolve, and his gait was majestic, like that of a royal elephant. His luminous face, framed by eyes as soft and serene as lotus petals, carried a gentle smile. Standing tall at about 8 feet, his presence was marked by a noble bearing and a well-built physique. Often, his divine aura is depicted with an emerald green hue.

However, since his separation from Devi Sita, sorrow had clouded Rama's visage. His lotus-petal eyes, once brimming with serenity, now frequently welled up with tears of sorrow. The smile that once enchanted the hearts of devotees and sages alike, had vanished.

Today, as Lord Rama listened intently to Sugreeva's assurances, hope flickered faintly within him. Sugreeva spoke with conviction, bolstered by the unmistakable energy of the returning Vanaras, a clear sign of their mission's success.

As the jubilant Vanara sena arrived, each one paid their respects to their king, Rama and Lakshmana. Their radiant auras spoke of triumph and joy.

Yet, the moment that Lord Rama had been yearning for was delivered by his greatest devotee. As Shri Ramadoot, the paragon of devotion, knelt before his Lord, who was seated upon a stone slab, he broke the conventional rules of grammar to convey his message succinctly and profoundly:

'Found Devi Sita, I...'

The divine brothers, whose faces were marred by the sorrow of separation and whose eyes bore the scars of endless tears, suddenly found a reservoir of relief as Hanuman spoke. Tears cascaded down their lotus-like faces as their pent-up anxiety and despair were washed away. Eyes brimming with tears yet sparkling with love, Rama, overcome with emotion, bestowed a heartfelt smile on Maruti, his beloved devotee.

Eager for more, Lord Rama inquired urgently, 'Is Sita alive? Does she remember me?'

Vayuputra, understanding the deep, spiritual bond that united this divine couple, reassured him, 'Janaki lives by the strength of her constant remembrance of you, and with the hope that she may soon behold you again. Not a moment passes when Ma does not think of you, dear Lord.'

As the other Vanaras chimed in, they shared the harsh realities of Devi Sita's captivity: her suffering among monstrous demonesses, her resilience in the gloomy Ashoka Grove, and Ravana's ceaseless threats. Goswami Tulsidas highlights that Jambavan specifically praised Hanuman for ensuring their survival by fulfilling this critical mission.

While Rama patiently listened to each narrative, his gaze remained fixed on his devoted servant, prompting Hanuman to delve deeper into his encounter with Sita.

Shri Hanuman, with characteristic humility, briefly recounted his perilous journey across the ocean to Lanka, focusing on what mattered most to Lord Rama—news of Sita.

'Amidst the vile demonesses and relentless torment from Ravana, she clings to austere practices to sustain her spirit. Surrounded by darkness, the radiant princess yearns for the joy of your divine companionship,' Shri Ramadoot relayed.

When I presented your ring to her, Hanuman continued, 'Devi Sita wept with joy, holding it close to her heart.'

He then presented a precious hair ornament (चूड़ामणि), as undeniable proof of their meeting.

'Sita also recounted an intimate memory from Chitrakoot (Kakasura)—a tale known only to you and her,' Hanuman said.

As Rama clutched the ornament, a feeble smile graced his lips as he reminisced about his father-in-law, the one who had given this precious gift to Sita on their wedding day.

Lord Rama's voice trembled with emotion as he addressed Hanuman, saying 'Dear Hanuman, this ornament you have given me is not just a piece of jewellery. It is a portal to my past, a connection to my beloved Janaki and my noble father-in-law, King Janaka. As I gaze upon this jewel, I feel as if I am in her presence once more.'

'Speak on, O Mahavir. The more you recount, the more my soul thirsts for tales of my beloved Janaki,' implored Rama.

Shri Hanuman echoed Sita's poignant query: 'Ma asks what stops you from employing a celestial weapon to finish off the menace of Ravana and rescuing me?

'Even all the gods and celestial army combined cannot defeat you in battle, O Rama! Why is my valorous brother-in-law not coming along with his venerable brother to release me from my unbearable misery?'

What will Shri Rama's heartfelt response be to this profound plea? How will this sacred dialogue between deity and devotee, master and servant, Vishnu and Rudra, continue to unfold?

Key Takeaway
Communicating Mindfully & Consciously
When Lord Rama had first met Hanuman, he praised him by telling Lakshmana that this person is so erudite and scholarly that I cannot find even one defect in his speech or grammar. However, Hanuman's seemingly grammatically incorrect statement, 'Found Devi Sita I,' holds a deeper meaning that requires context to fully comprehend.

Shri Hanuman could have simply said:
I found Devi Sita
Or
Devi Sita was found.
Or
Mission accomplished.

The scholars and acharyas of the Ramayana reveal that there was a profound reason for Maruti's statement.

Shri Hanuman whose life is about service, particularly to Rama, knew exactly what the Lord was aching to hear.

He had previously witnessed the intense anxiety, pain and

worry that Lord Rama went through. He was also mindful that their search party was already late in arriving back and now all he wished to do was to ensure Rama hears the words—found! That was what the mission was all about finding Sita. That was what Raghunath's ears ached to hear. That's all that he was endeavouring—to find his beloved wife ever since she'd been abducted.

The fact that Maruti had achieved such a mammoth task didn't matter; what mattered was the mission was completed. It was not Hanuman who achieved it, but the grace of his beloved Lord and gods that led him to attain success. Therefore, in his first sentence to Rama on reaching him, *I* came last.

And any intelligent, conscious being desirous of enduring success should keep *I* or the ego last, while keeping their duty, work, and God on the forefront.

While Lord Hanuman didn't talk about the details of his journey and adventures to Shri Rama, he did mention about it to his fellow Vanara soldiers as he wanted to instil hope and self-belief in them.

Shri Hanuman, a master communicator, serves as a reminder that effective communication is a universal skill. It's not just for those in leadership positions or those whose work requires frequent interaction. We all can benefit from improving our ability to express ourselves clearly and understand others. Whether it's in our personal relationships, professional endeavours, or even in our daily interactions, communication is a fundamental tool for success and happiness.

All too often, relationships are lost due to misunderstandings caused by poor communication. On the other hand, relationships are also built and strengthened through open and honest conversations.

When to speak, what to speak and how to speak is something each and every individual should endeavour to learn.

Lord Hanuman and the *Sundar Kand* teach us:
To be sensitive with your words.
To use your words to uplift, and to inspire.
To use your good sense to speak what is most beneficial for everyone.
To speak in a way that is concise and precise.
And most definitely, not prattle on continuously about yourself!

We all love to talk about ourselves. But if everyone is only interested in talking, who will even listen? Often conversations end up becoming a competition about who can talk more rather than listening patiently and responding.

We see here that Shri Hanuman shares the most important bit of information and then stays silent. Only when he realises Rama intends him to elaborate does he start speaking in detail. And Lord Rama, on his part, listens patiently without interrupting his dear Hanuman.

A life-long lesson that we can take away from this epic story is that one who can communicate mindfully and consciously will be endearing to everyone around.

Your Reflection

Have you ever delivered happy news to someone? It could be even something like you attaining a good result in your exams to your parents.

Reflect back on that time, or better yet, think if there was a time you delivered news that another person was eagerly waiting for, and you were the blessed medium to deliver that. Journal how that made you feel.

Additionally, you can reflect, what can you learn and derive from Lord Hanuman's communication skills? How did he manage to convey his messages effectively? How can you better your communication by adopting some of his techniques?

नाथ पवनसुत कीन्हि जो करनी । सहसहुँ मुख न जाइ सो बरनी ॥

Jambavan: O Lord, the glory of the incredible feat of Hanuman cannot even be encapsulated if I had a thousand mouths to speak.

Chapter 3
Ramadoot Becomes Rama Das

Lord Hanuman continued to share more, addressing Devi Sita's concerns about the seemingly insurmountable challenge of crossing the vast ocean and confronting the formidable *Rakshasa* army.

Mahavir reassured Raghunath, 'If a humble servant like myself could traverse the ocean, then certainly the rest of Sugreeva's army, each as capable if not more so than I, can also leap across and vanquish the demons. I assured Devi Sita that Shri Rama, Lakshmana, along with Sugreeva and the Vanara army, would soon eradicate the symbols of injustice and sin.'

Hearing these humble words, Lord Rama smiled lovingly at the Rudra Avatar. He was well aware that none but Hanuman could have achieved this daunting task. It was no coincidence that the Lord had entrusted him with the ring; Rama knew only Hanuman could reach Sita.

Shri Ramadoot recounted how he had implored Devi Sita to return with him, an offer she declined not out of reluctance but from a desire to see her divine husband triumph over evil, to ensure the world witnessed the might of Lord Rama and learned a stern lesson about the consequences of transgressing *dharma*.

The revelation of such profound love left the Vanaras in awe, their expressions a mix of wonder and disbelief at the depth and purity of the bond between Sita and Rama.

Lord Rama was overwhelmed with a torrent of emotions; the echo of Sita's words, carried by Hanuman, filled him with immense love and poignant grief. Her selflessness shone brilliantly, prioritising Rama's honour above her own dire circumstances.

Reflecting on Hanuman's extraordinary achievements, Lord Rama declared that none but Garuda—the mighty celestial bird and carrier of Bhagvan Shri Vishnu—or Vayu himself could have navigated the vast ocean. And only Hanuman, with his unmatched wisdom and sensitivity, could have penetrated the defences of Lanka to reach Sita.

With boundless gratitude, Shri Rama proclaimed, 'My clan and I will forever remain indebted to you, O Hanuman.'

'There is nothing I can offer that matches the magnitude of your service. All I can give is my heartfelt, loving embrace,' Lord Rama said, extending his arms towards his devotee.

What more could a devotee desire than the loving embrace of his Lord?

Overwhelmed by emotion, Shri Ramadoot fell at the feet of Lord Rama, clinging to the refuge of his lotus feet, despite Raghunath's gentle attempts to raise him. It was only when Lord Rama tenderly stroked his head that Hanuman was lifted into the divine embrace.

Tulsidas, a saint of the highest bhakti order, notes that in this moment, Hanuman sought the ultimate blessing of unwavering devotion to Paramatma Shri Rama.

The entire assembly was enveloped in a wave of divine love, tears of admiration and joy welling up in their eyes. They recognised that the grace bestowed upon Hanuman was what mystics, saints, and yogis aspired to across countless lifetimes of austerity.

Holding his devotee's hands, Shri Rama, intrigued by Hanuman's feats in Lanka, asked, 'Tell me, how did you manage to set aflame the formidable city of Lanka?'

Key Takeaway
Be Kind in Word and Deed
It's a common misconception that ultimate fulfilment lies in the acquisition of objects or the accumulation of material wealth. Our scriptures and life's wisdom teach us different truths—that the ultimate fulfilment is found in selfless service to people we love and to society at large. We wish to serve, one way or another.

Some wish to only serve their interests and lead miserable lives within, no matter how abundant their life looks from the outside, while others look to serve their loved ones and family members, often undergoing sacrifice to bring joy for others.

As I keep growing older and growing through life, I have fortunately and blessedly understood that the greatest gift that one can gain is the joy of good relationships. The happiness that is attained on seeing your loved ones feel joy because of your deeds or words is the ultimate fulfilment. Consider the case of Shri Hanuman, whose most cherished gift was a hug from Lord Rama. The sheer joy he experienced from being deeply appreciated is a testament to the power of gratitude in our lives.

Of course, a very important point here is that both Lord Rama and Hanuman are reciprocative towards each other. And more so, both of the divine personalities are content within.

Put simply, in the realm of interpersonal relationships, we cannot find true fulfillment if our efforts go unnoticed. It's not about seeking constant praise, but about the basic human need for acknowledgment. Without it, we may find ourselves in a state of unfulfilment, even depression.

When I speak of inner fulfilment, I emphasise the importance of self-care. It's about ensuring our own cup is full of contentment and positivity. Only with such a cup can we even think of pouring out kind and loving service to others.

We cannot imitate divine personalities or need to fulfil a herculean task or should be now call it a Hanumanian task to serve others. It can be through the smallest kind gesture, a loving word or a sincere heartfelt prayer for their wellbeing—something like, 'may this person be happy, fulfilled, and healthy.'

Your Reflection

Has there been a moment and time in your life journey when you felt overwhelmed with tears of gratitude? Who or what has touched your life in the most profound way?

बार बार प्रभु चहइ उठावा । प्रेम मगन तेहि उठब न भावा ॥
प्रभु कर पंकज कपि कें सीसा । सुमिरि सो दसा मगन गौरीसा ॥

The lord kept trying to lift up Hanuman, but so deeply immersed was he in love that he wouldn't budge. Recalling the state and scene of Shri Rama lovingly stroke the head of Hanuman, Bhagavan Shiva entered a yogic trance.

Chapter 4

No Reason to Delay

Shri Hanuman, in his humility, had initially withheld the details of his exploits in Lanka. After delivering Devi Sita's message, a profound exchange of love and surrender unfolded between God and devotee. Curious, Lord Rama asked his beloved Hanuman to recount how he managed to burn down the heavily fortified city of Lanka.

प्रभु प्रसन्न जाना हनुमाना । बोला बचन बिगत अभिमाना ॥

Delighted to have pleased his Lord, Shri Hanuman spoke words devoid of ego or pride.

'For Vanaras, leaping from one tree branch to another is the norm; but for me to cross the ocean and set Lanka ablaze was merely a reflection of your divine grace,' said Shri Rama Das.

Shri Hanuman detailed his devastation of the Ashoka Grove and strategic sites within Lanka.

'No credit belongs to me, my Lord; it is all Your grace. When you favour someone, nothing is impossible for them. Your grace transforms the impossible into the possible.'

Overwhelmed with compassion and love, the benevolent Lord Rama could only respond by showering his divine light of love on his devoted servant. Hanuman then vividly described

Lanka's formidable military strength, its robust fortifications, and the might of the *Rakshasas*. Despite his destructive efforts, he cautioned everyone that by the time Lord Rama's army arrived, the enemy would likely have rebuilt and fortified the city even more robustly. He emphasised that threats should never be underestimated.

Deep in contemplation, Lord Rama weighed Hanuman's words. The urgency of Sita's one-month deadline pressed on him, calling for swift and decisive action.

Sugreeva, brimming with confidence, proposed constructing a bridge across the ocean. Assertive and positive, the Vanara king assured everyone of their eventual victory, buoyed by auspicious omens.

Inspired by Sugreeva's unwavering faith, Lord Rama resolutely declared, 'We shall not delay. Whether by bridge, mystical power, or even drying the ocean if necessary, I am determined to lead our forces to Lanka. The stars align favourably, and the time is right; let us march forth. Ravana's days are numbered.'

Lord Rama's proclamation ignited a resounding cheer among the Vanaras. As he cast a loving glance at them, the divine Lord infused them with renewed power, energy, grace, and blessings.

Sugreeva then tasked Nila, his commander, with leading a vanguard to the south to prevent an ambush. The mightiest warriors, Gaja, Dvividha, Mainda, and others took the lead, while Lord Rama, Lakshmana, Angad, Sugreeva, Jambavan, and Hanuman, formed the heart of the march towards the southern shore. This assembly was on the brink of creating history—a saga so magnificent that it would be celebrated and retold for millennia.

Shri Ramachandra Bhagavan kee Jai! Shri Ramadoot Hanuman kee Jai!

Key Takeaway
Seek God's Grace in all that We Do
The most important and pertinent lesson we can draw from this episode is that with God's grace, even the impossible can be achieved with ease and harmony.

Just like the devotees offer Ma Ganga's waters back to her as an offering, we too should offer our activities and work to God as an offering of our love. With such an attitude, even the most mundane act can be spiritualised, leading to success, contentment, and joy in this life and ahead.

सो सब तव प्रताप रघुराई । नाथ न कछू मोरि प्रभुताई ॥

Even in the contemporary world, we witness that those who have achieved the pinnacle of success have attributed it to more than just their ability and talent.

Virat Kohli, a stalwart of the Indian Cricket team, unleashed a shot of unparalleled brilliance against a Pakistani bowler in the T20 World Cup of 2022. This shot, a true masterpiece, was rightfully hailed as the 'ICC Shot of the century'. Later when asked about the stroke, Kohli said it seemed like something took over him that moment; as if some divine force propelled him to hit that jaw dropping shot.

Among those who consistently achieve greatness, there is a common thread—an unwavering commitment, a relentless pursuit of excellence. But perhaps more intriguingly, there is also a sense of surrender, a recognition of a higher power at play.

Your Reflection

Think about your connection to what you call God, higher consciousness, spirit, universe, or Bhagavan. When have you felt most connected to divinity?

And last, what has been your biggest takeaway from Shri Hanuman's story in the book?

उमा राम सुभाउ जेहिं जाना। ताहि भजनु तजि भाव न आना॥

Addressing Ma Parvati, Bhagavan Shiva says those who know the true nature of Shri Rama, they can't help but sing his glories.

Concluding Words

There is a special book called *The Adhyatma Ramayana* which comes under an ancient text known as *Brahmanda Purana*, authored by Krishna Dvaipayana Vyasa. It mentions that Sita represents the soul, or *Jivatma* that has been separated from Rama or *Paramatma*. Hanuman represents *bhakti* that can annihilate the ego symbolised by Ravana to unite *Atma* and *Paramatma*.

If you have stayed with me and the story thus far, I thank you immensely for your time and effort to read through the book. It is my sincere belief and prayer that anyone who sincerely reads Shri Hanuman's story will experience some form of miracle in their life. I most certainly did during the course of writing this book!

Sundar Kand, the book of beauty, will bestow upon you both inner and outer beauty, wisdom, inner strength and grace.

I tried narrating a tale that is dearest to my heart in the most simple words. I have precious little spiritual experience or insight. My command over the English language and expression is still a work in progress. However, I have tried to share this story with utmost honour, respect and sincerity.

Whenever I write, my approach and intent is that it should

help at least one person beyond me. Writing this has been one of the most satisfying and biggest achievements of my life. If it helps one more person beyond me, it will make my journey of writing this story even more gratifying.

If you liked any thing about this book, I humbly request you to write a review on Amazon and Goodreads.

You can also directly connect to me on my email: kenshosandsatoris@gmail.com

For those interested in taking their journey further, in the next section, I have shared some tools that can help us in establishing a connection with Lord Hanuman and be a recipient of his grace.

More than anything, I hope this tiny effort of mine inspires you to read the original source—the Ramayana itself.

बुद्धिर् बलम् यशो धैर्यम्
निर्भयत्वम् अरोगताम्
अजाद्यम् वाक् पटुत्वम् च
हनुमत् स्मरणात् भवेत् ॥

By contemplating on the character of Hanuman, one gains intelligence, strength, fame, patience, good health, fearlessness, and skilful speech.

May you be blessed with all this and more.

Connecting with Lord Hanuman *(Sadhna)*

Goswami Tulsidas is considered to be a reincarnation of Maharishi Valmiki. It is said, Shri Valmiki returned primarily to glorify Hanuman prominently.

Tulsidas has given us beautiful hymns to seek the grace and blessings of Shri Hanuman. Almost every devout Hindu knows or has read the *Hanuman Chalisa* at least once. One can also read *Sankat Mochan Hanuman Ashtak* as well.

Hanuman Chalisa can be a daily ritual that is easy to do and can give a lot of blessings and protection to the seeker or *sadhak*. It takes around 2-3 minutes only to complete the chant. Always begin your chanting post a shower and light up a lamp. If possible, always use a wool *asana* (seat or clothing) dedicated only for worship or devotional activities.

Sankat Mochan Hanuman Astak is specially useful in times of need and when you're looking for a special intervention by Lord Hanuman.

Another time-tested and potent solution to almost any kind of problem is to chant 108 rounds of *Hanuman Chalisa* in one go. This can be employed in desperate times to surrender completely and fully to Lord Hanuman. The gracious Ramadoot will definitely ensure you overcome any issue that you are going through.

This method is also prescribed within the *Hanuman Chalisa*:
जो सत बार पाठ कर कोई।
छूटहि बंदि महा सुख होई॥

Always begin and conclude any *sadhna* of Lord Hanuman with chants of *Shri Sita Rama*. Post this, sit for a minute or two meditating upon the beautiful, gentle form of Shri Hanuman bestowing his blessings on you.

No planetary shifts, negativity or trouble can overcome a sincere devotee of Shri Ramadoot because that person not just gets the blessings of Lord Hanuman but also of Sita, Rama, and Lakshmana. You need not consult any guide, astrologer or approach a healer if you can cultivate sincere faith in the name of Rama and the power of Ramadoot.

As Goswami says:
और देवता चित्त न धरई।
हनुमत सेइ सर्ब सुख करई॥

Hanuman's worship is sufficient to attain joy and success.

A word of caution here: Any worship of Lord Hanuman or Vishnu Tattva or avataras of Bhagavan Shri Vishnu requires one to adopt a *sattvik* lifestyle. In other words, one must give up meat, alcohol and illicit sexual activities to attain the full benefit of worship.

One can also try and read *Sundar Kand* of Goswami Tulsidas. With practice, one can complete one reading in about 30-40 minutes. Or one can keep reading a few couplets daily. Even that can act as a wonderful tool to stay connected with Shri Hanuman and receive his and Lord Rama's blessings.

Offering *Sindoor*

You would have noticed that that many deities of Shri Hanuman are covered in orange vermillion from head to toe. That is the most popular manifestation of Lord Hanuman in almost every temple, especially up north of Bharat.

Legend goes that once in Ayodhya, Shri Hanuman noticed Devi Sita applying vermillion on her forehead, as every married woman applies in Sanatan Dharma. When he enquired why did she do so, she said it was to invoke protection and for a long and prosperous life for Lord Rama.

The innocent Maruti went to the market and got a large amount of vermillion. He poured it all over his body and entered Lord Rama's court. Seeing the Mahavir inundated with vermillion from head to toe evoked peals of laughter from the court. Lord Rama, however, waited for his dear devotee to offer an explanation. Vajrangi said he got the idea from Devi Sita.

'If applying a tiny amount can offer protection and invoke auspiciousness, why don't I pour vermillion all over my body?' Maruti said. The innocence and devotion of Hanuman delighted the heart of Lord Rama who embraced his devotee with love.

Remembering this pastime, one can offer *sindoor* to Lord Hanuman. This is particularly done on Tuesdays to help one channelise the effects of the Mars planet positively, as an astrological remedy. Mars as a planet is considered to be harsh in nature and can cause trouble for one who is afflicted by its influence in their birth chart.

Additionally, Lord Hanuman is one of the very few deities who can help one overcome the harsh tests of Saturn. It is said, Shani Dev offered immunity to one who worships Hanuman from his harsh gaze. The moral is that anyone who works to inculcate the following attributes is able to overcome any sort of challenge:

1. Discipline
2. Sincere endeavour
3. Focus
4. Gratitude as an attitude in life
5. Belief in oneself and God
6. Humility
7. Surrendering their activities to the divine

If you reflect back on our story, this is all that the book tries to present. If one is armed with these attributes, success is most certainly assured.

Mantra for Manifesting Help
कवन सो काज कठिन जग माहीं । जो नहिं होइ तात तुम्ह पाहीं ॥

This verse from the *Kishkinda Kanda*, as chanted by Jambavan to Lord Hanuman is a potent mantra if someone seeks help for any issue in their life. You can use this verse as a mantra, meditating on Shri Hanuman's divine capability to help out in any issue that you face in life.

Mantra for Success
प्रबिसि नगर कीजे सब काजा । हृदयँ राखि कोसलपुर राजा ॥

This potent verse appears in the *Sundar Kanda* when Hanuman is entering Lanka. It was discussed in the book as well. You can chant this verse meditating on your desire for success in any endeavour. By the blessings of Lord Rama and Ramadoot, you will definitely find success and accomplishment.

Mantra to Chant Before Travelling (and Sleeping)
There is a special mantra containing 12 names of Lord Hanuman that one can chant before leaving for a trip or any kind of travel to invoke protection. You can also use this mantra before bed time in case you are going through troubled sleep or having bad dreams. This mantra is the *Hanuman Dwadash Naam Stotram*.

हनुमानंजनासूनुः वायुपुत्रो महाबलः। रामेष्टः फल्गुणसखः पिंगाक्षोऽमितविक्रमः॥ १॥
उदधिक्रमणश्चैव सीताशोकविनाशकः। लक्ष्मण प्राणदाताच दशग्रीवस्य दर्पहा॥ २॥
द्वादशैतानि नामानि कपींद्रस्य महात्मनः। स्वापकाले पठेन्नित्यं यात्राकाले विशेषतः।
तस्यमृत्यु भयंनास्ति सर्वत्र विजयी भवेत् ॥

Suggested Reading

- *Ramayana Retold* by Krishna Dharma: One of the best retellings of the Ramayana available in the contemporary world. *Krishna Dharma* gives an authentic narration in simple language.
- *Hanuman Chalisa* by Shubh Vilas: The author narrates one story connected to each verse of the *Hanuman Chalisa*. This book is an amazing resource to help us connect more with the grace of Shri Hanuman.
- *The Ramayana series* (6 books) by Shubh Vilas also gives an in-depth study of the epic of the Ramayana. Written in an engaging style and full of reflective lessons, this is an amazing read.
- *Hanuman: The Devotion and Power of the Monkey God* by Vanamali. This is a beautiful, succinct resource on the character, activities and life of Lord Hanuman.
- Valmikiramayana.net proved really useful in my research and study of the *Valmiki Ramayana*. You can study the original scripture through this authentic online resource.

- *Ramacharitmanas (and Sundar Kand)* by Goswami Tulsidas brings in auspiciousness, joy, well-being and abundance, *Ramacharitmanas* is a potent resource and manifestation of Shri Rama's grace. Any sincere bhakti yogi can derive immense benefit from reading this epic by Tulsidas.